His
the arians

Athanasius of Alexandria

book published by
LIMOVIA.NET

TWITTER: @EBOOKLIMOVIA

isbn: 978-1490479729

Therefore anyone who sets aside one of the least of these commands and teaches others accordingly will be called least in the kingdom of heaven, but whoever practices and teaches these commands will be called great in the kingdom of heaven.

Matthew 5:19

The author: Athanasius of Alexandria

Athanasius of Alexandria (Greek: Ἀθανάσιος Ἀλεξανδρείας, Athanásios Alexandrías) (b. ca. 296-298 – d. 2 May 373), also referred to as St. Athanasius the Great, St. Athanasius I of Alexandria, St Athanasius the Confessor and (primarily in the Coptic Orthodox Church) St Athanasius the Apostolic, was the 20th bishop of Alexandria. His episcopate lasted 45 years (c. 8 June 328 – 2 May 373), of which over 17 were spent in five exiles ordered by four different Roman emperors. He is considered to be a renowned Christian theologian, a Church Father, the chief defender of Trinitarianism against Arianism, and a noted Egyptian leader of the fourth century.

He is remembered for his role in the conflict with Arius and Arianism. In 325, at the age of 27, Athanasius had a leading role against the Arians in the First Council of Nicaea. At the time, he was a deacon and personal secretary of the 19th Bishop of Alexandria, Alexander. Nicaea was convoked by Constantine I in May–August 325 to address the Arian position that Jesus of Nazareth is of a distinct substance from the Father.

In June 328, at the age of 30, three years after Nicæa and upon the repose of Bishop Alexander, he became archbishop of Alexandria. He continued to lead the conflict against the Arians for the rest of his life and was engaged in theological and political struggles against the Emperors Constantine the Great and Constantius II and powerful and influential Arian churchmen, led by Eusebius of Nicomedia and others. He was known as "Athanasius Contra Mundum". Within a few years of his departure, St. Gregory of Nazianzus called him the "Pillar of the Church". His writings were well regarded by all Church fathers who followed, in both the West and the East. His writings show a rich devotion to the Word-become-man, great pastoral concern, and profound interest in monasticism.

Athanasius is counted as one of the four great Eastern Doctors of the Church in the Roman Catholic Church and in Eastern Orthodoxy, he is labeled the "Father of Orthodoxy". He is also celebrated by many Protestants, who label him "Father of The Canon". Athanasius is venerated as a Christian saint, whose feast day is 2 May in Western Christianity, 15 May in the Coptic Orthodox Church, and 18 January in the other Eastern Orthodox Churches. He is venerated by the Roman Catholic Church, Oriental and Eastern Orthodox churches, the Lutherans, and the Anglican Communion.

St Athanasius was born in the city of Alexandria or possibly the nearby Nile Delta town of Damanhur ca. 296-298. It is speculated that his parents were wealthy enough to afford giving him an esteemed secular learning. In his earliest work, Against the Heathen - On the Incarnation, written before 319, he repeatedly quoted Plato and used a definition from the Organon of Aristotle. He was also familiar with the theories of various philosophical schools, and in particular with the developments of Neo-Platonism. In later works, he quotes Homer more than once (Hist. Ar. 68, Orat. iv. 29). In his letter to Emperor Constantius, he presents a defense of himself bearing unmistakable traces of a study of Demosthenes de Corona (Fialon).

He came from a Christian family, despite accounts to the contrary, as in his writings he tells more than once of an aunt who taught him some principles of the Christian faith, and a father who did the same, as well as mentioning (once) his mother doing the same. He had a Christian brother, and later in his life, in one of his exiles, he hid in his father's tomb in what appears[citation needed] to be described as a Christian cemetery.

He knew Greek and he admits to not knowing Hebrew [see, e.g., the 39th Festal Letter of St. Athan.]. The Old Testament passages he quotes frequently come from the Septuagint Greek translation. Ignorant of Hebrew, and only rarely appealing to other Greek versions (to Aquila once in the Ecthesis, to other versions once or twice on the Psalms), his knowledge of the Old Testament is limited to the Septuagint.[3] He was able to write a letter in exile, with no access to a copy of the Scriptures, and quote from memory every verse in the Old Testament with reference to the Trinity without missing any. The combination of Scriptural study and of Greek learning was characteristic of the famous Alexandrian School, of Clement, Origen, Dionysius and Theognostus.

At the time he was a student, the influence of Origen was still felt in the traditions of the theological school of Alexandria. It was from St. Alexander of Alexandria, Bishop of Alexandria, 312–328, himself an Origenist, that St Athanasius received his main instruction. His earliest work,Against the Heathen - On the Incarnation, bears traces of Origenist Alexandrian thought but in an orthodox way. He later modified the philosophical thought of the School of Alexandria away from the Origenist principles such as the "entirely allegorical interpretation of the text" proposed by Origen.

The Alexandria of his boyhood was an epitome—intellectually, morally, and politically—of the ethnically diverse Graeco-Roman world. It was the most important center of trade in the whole empire; and its primacy as an emporium of ideas was more commanding than that of Rome or Constantinople, Antioch or Marseilles. Its famous catechetical school, while sacrificing none of its famous passion for orthodoxy since the days of Pantaenus, Clement of Alexandria, and Origen of Alexandria, had begun to take on an almost secular character in the comprehensiveness of its interests, and had counted influential pagans among its serious auditors.

St Athanasius seems to have been brought early in life under the immediate supervision of the ecclesiastical authorities of his native city. A story has been preserved by Rufinus (Hist. Eccl., I, xiv). Bishop Alexander, so the tale runs, had invited a number of fellow prelates to meet him at breakfast after a great religious function. While Alexander was waiting for his guests to arrive, he stood by a window, watching a group of boys at play on the seashore below the house. He had not observed them long before he discovered that they were imitating the elaborate ritual of Christian baptism. He sent for the children and, in the investigation that followed, it was discovered that one of the boys (none other than Athanasius) had acted the part of the bishop and in that character had actually baptized several of his companions in the course of their play. Alexander determined to recognize the make-believe baptisms as genuine, and decided that Athanasius and his playfellows should go into training in order to prepare themselves for a clerical career.

Sozomen speaks of his "fitness for the

priesthood", and calls attention to the significant circumstance that he was "from his tenderest years practically self-taught". "Not long after this," adds the same authority, Bishop Alexander "invited Athanasius to be his commensal and secretary. He had been well educated, and was versed in grammar and rhetoric, and had already, while still a young man, and before reaching the episcopate, given proof to those who dwelt with him of his wisdom and acumen" (Soz., II, xvii). That "wisdom and acumen" manifested themselves in a varied environment. While still a deacon under Alexander's care, he seems to have been brought for a while into close relations with some of the solitaries of the Egyptian desert, and in particular with the Anthony the Great, whose life he is said to have written.

He was ordained a deacon by the contemporary patriarch, Alexander of Alexandria, in 319. In 325, he served as Alexander's secretary at the First Council of Nicaea. Already a recognized theologian and ascetic, he was the obvious choice to replace Alexander as the Patriarch of Alexandria on the latter's death in 328, despite the opposition of the followers of Arius and Meletius of Lycopolis.

Athanasius spent the first years of his

patriarchate visiting the churches of his territory, which at that time included all of Egypt and Libya. During this period, he established contacts with the hermits and monks of the desert, including Pachomius, which would be very valuable to him over the years. Shortly thereafter, Athanasius became occupied with the disputes with the Byzantine Empire and Arians which would occupy much of his life.

Athanasius' first problem lay with the Meletians, who had failed to abide by the terms of the decision made at the First Council of Nicaea which had hoped to reunite them with the Church. Athanasius himself was accused of mistreating Arians and the followers of Meletius of Lycopolis, and had to answer those charges at a gathering of bishops in Tyre, the First Synod of Tyre, in 335. At that meeting, Eusebius of Nicomedia and the other supporters of Arius deposed Athanasius. On 6 November, both parties of the dispute met with Constantine I in Constantinople. At that meeting, Athanasius was accused of threatening to interfere with the supply of grains from Egypt, and, without any kind of formal trial, was exiled by Constantine to Trier in the Rhineland.

On the death of Emperor Constantine I,

Athanasius was allowed to return to his See of Alexandria. Shortly thereafter, however, Constantine's son, the new Roman Emperor Constantius II, renewed the order for Athanasius' banishment in 338. Athanasius went to Rome, where he was under the protection of Constans, the Emperor of the West. During this time, Gregory of Cappadocia was installed as the Patriarch of Alexandria, usurping the absent Athanasius. Athanasius did, however, remain in contact with his people through his annual Festal Letters, in which he also announced on which date Easter would be celebrated that year.

Pope Julius I wrote to the supporters of Arius strongly urging the reinstatement of Athanasius, but that effort proved to be in vain. He called a synod in Rome in the year 341 to address the matter, and at that meeting Athanasius was found to be innocent of all the charges raised against him. Julius also called the Council of Sardica in 343. This council confirmed the decision of the earlier Roman synod, and clearly indicated that the participants saw St Athanasius as the lawful Patriarch of Alexandria. It proved no more successful, however, as only bishops from the West and Egypt bothered to appear.

"Early in the year 343, Athanasius went to Gaul, whither he had gone to consult the saintly Hosius of Corduba, the great champion of orthodoxy in the West. The two together set out for the Council of Sardica which had been summoned in deference to the Roman pontiff's wishes. At this great gathering of prelates the case of Athanasius was taken up and once more his innocence reaffirmed. Two conciliar letters were prepared, one to the clergy and faithful of Alexandria, the other to the bishops of Egypt and Libya, in which the will of the Council was made known. The persecution against the orthodox party broke out with renewed vigor, and Constantius II was induced to prepare drastic measures against Athanasius and the priests who were devoted to him. Orders were given that if the Saint attempted to re-enter his episcopal see, he should be put to death."

In 346, following the death of Gregory, Constans used his influence to allow Athanasius to return to Alexandria. Athanasius' return was welcomed by the majority of the people of Egypt who had come to view him as a national hero. This was the start of a "golden decade" of peace and prosperity, during which time Athanasius assembled several documents relating to his exiles and returns from exile in the Apology Against the Arians. However, upon Constans' death in 350, a civil war broke out which left Constantius as sole emperor. Constantius, renewing his previous policies favoring the Arians, banished Athanasius from Alexandria once again. This was followed, in 356, by an attempt to arrest Athanasius during a vigil service. Following this, Athanasius left for Upper Egypt, where he stayed in several monasteries and other houses. During this period, Athanasius completed his work Four Orations against the Arians and defended his own recent conduct in the Apology to Constantius and Apology for His Flight. Constantius' persistence in his opposition to Athanasius, combined with reports Athanasius received about the persecution of non-Arians by the new Arian bishop George of Laodicea, prompted Athanasius to write his more emotional History of the Arians, in which he described Constantius as a precursor of the Antichrist.

In 361, after the death of Emperor Constantius, shortly followed by the murder of the very unpopular Bishop George, the popular St Athanasius now had the opportunity to return to his patriarchate. The following year he convened a council at Alexandria at which he appealed for unity among all those who had faith in Christianity, even if they differed on matters of terminology. This prepared the groundwork for the definition of the orthodox doctrine of the Trinity. In 362, the new Emperor Julian, noted for his opposition to Christianity, ordered Athanasius to leave Alexandria once again. Athanasius left for Upper Egypt, remaining there until Julian's death in 363. Two years later, the Emperor Valens, who favored the Arian position, in his turn exiled Athanasius. This time however, Athanasius simply left for the outskirts of Alexandria, where he stayed for only a few months before the local authorities convinced Valens to retract his order of exile. Some of the early reports explicitly indicate that Athanasius spent this period of exile in his ancestral tomb.

Valens, who seems to have sincerely dreaded the possible consequences of a popular outbreak, gave orders within a few weeks for the return of Athanasius to his episcopal see. Here, St Athanasius, spent his remaining days, characteristically enough, in re-emphasizing the view of the Incarnation which had been defined at Nicaea. He died peacefully in his own bed, surrounded by his clergy and faithful.

History of the arians ~ Athanasius of Alexandria

BOOK I

Arian Persecution Under Constantine

And not long after they put in execution the designs for the sake of which they had had recourse to these artifices; for they no sooner had formed their plans, but they immediately admitted Arius and his fellows to communion. They set aside the repeated condemnations which had been passed upon them, and again pretended the imperial authority in their behalf. And they were not ashamed to say in their letters, 'since Athanasius suffered, all jealousy has ceased, and let us henceforward receive Arius and his fellows;' adding, in order to frighten their hearers, 'because the Emperor has commanded it.' Moreover, they were not ashamed to add, 'for these men profess orthodox opinions;' not fearing that which is written, 'Woe unto them that call bitter sweet, that put darkness for light Isaiah 5:20;' for they are ready to undertake anything in support of their heresy. Now is it not hereby plainly proved to all men, that we both suffered heretofore, and that you now persecute us, not under the authority of an Ecclesiastical sentence , but on the ground of the Emperor's threats, and on account of our piety towards Christ? As also they conspired in like manner against other Bishops, fabricating charges against them also; some of whom fell asleep in the place of their exile, having attained the glory of Christian confession; and others are still banished from their country, and contend still more and more manfully against their heresy, saying, 'Nothing shall separate us from the love of Christ Romans 8:35?'

Arianssacrifice morality and integrity to party

And hence also you may discern its character, and be able to condemn it more confidently. The man who is their friend and their associate in impiety, although he is open to ten thousand charges for other enormities which he has committed; although the evidence and proof against him are most clear; he is approved of by them, and straightway becomes the friend of the Emperor, obtaining an introduction by his impiety; and making very many pretences, he acquires confidence before the magistrates to do whatever he desires. But he who exposes their impiety, and honestly advocates the cause of Christ, though he is pure in all things, though he is conscious of no delinquencies, though he meets with no accuser; yet on the false pretences which they have framed against him, is immediately seized and sent into banishment under a sentence of the Emperor, as if he were guilty of the crimes which they wish to charge upon him, or as if, like Naboth, he had insulted the King; while he who advocates the cause of their heresy is sought for and immediately sent to take possession of the other's Church; and henceforth confiscations and insults, and all kinds of cruelty are exercised against those who do not receive him. And what is the strangest of all, the man whom the people desire, and know to be blameless 1 Timothy 3:2, the Emperor takes away and banishes; but him whom they neither desire, nor know, he sends to them from a distant place with soldiers and letters from himself. And henceforward a strong necessity is laid upon them, either to hate him whom they love; who has been their teacher, and their father in godliness; and to love him whom they do not desire, and to trust their children to one of whose life and conversation and character they are ignorant; or else certainly to suffer punishment, if they disobey the Emperor.

History of the arians ~ Athanasius of Alexandria

Recklessness of their proceedings

In this manner the impious are now proceeding, as heretofore, against the orthodox; giving proof of their malice and impiety among all men everywhere. For granting that they have accused Athanasius; yet what have the other Bishops done? On what grounds can they charge them? Has there been found in their case too the dead body of an Arsenius? Is there a Presbyter Macarius, or has a cup been broken among them? Is there a Meletian to play the hypocrite? No: but as their proceedings against the other Bishops show the charges which they have brought against Athanasius, in all probability, to be false; so their attacks upon Athanasius make it plain, that their accusations of the other Bishops are unfounded likewise. This heresy has come forth upon the earth like some great monster, which not only injures the innocent with its words, as with teeth ; but it has also hired external power to assist it in its designs. And strange it is that, as I said before, no accusation is brought against any of them; or if any be accused, he is not brought to trial; or if a show of enquiry be made, he is acquitted against evidence, while the convicting party is plotted against, rather than the culprit put to shame. Thus the whole party of them is full of idleness; and their spies, for Bishops they are not, are the vilest of them all. And if any one among them desire to become a Bishop, he is not told, 'a Bishop must be blameless 1

Timothy 3:2;' but only, 'Take up opinions contrary to Christ, and care not for manners. This will be sufficient to obtain favour for you, and friendship with the Emperor.' Such is the character of those who support the tenets of Arius. And they who are zealous for the truth, however holy and pure they show themselves, are yet, as I said before, made culprits, whenever these men choose, and on whatever pretences it may seem good to them to invent. The truth of this, as I before remarked, you may clearly gather from their proceedings.

Arianspersecute Eustathius and others

There was one Eustathius , Bishop of Antioch, a Confessor, and sound in the Faith. This man, because he was very zealous for the truth, and hated the Arian heresy, and would not receive those who adopted its tenets, is falsely accused before the Emperor Constantine, and a charge invented against him, that he had insulted his mother. And immediately he is driven into banishment, and a great number of Presbyters and Deacons with him. And immediately after the banishment of the Bishop, those whom he would not admit into the clerical order on account of their impiety were not only received into the Church by them, but were even appointed the greater part of them to be Bishops, in order that they might have accomplices in their impiety. Among these was Leontius the eunuch , now of Antioch, and his predecessor Stephanus, George of Laodicea, and Theodosius who was of Tripolis, Eudoxius of Germanicia, and Eustathius , now of Sebastia.

5. Did they then stop here? No. For Eutropius , who was Bishop of Adrianople, a good man, and excellent in all respects, because he had often convicted Eusebius, and had advised them who came that way, not to comply with his impious dictates, suffered the same treatment as Eustathius, and was cast out of his

city and his Church. Basilina was the most active in the proceedings against him. And Euphration of Balanea, Kymatius of Paltus, Carterius of Antaradus , Asclepas of Gaza, Cyrus of Berœa in Syria, Diodorus of Asia, Domnion of Sirmium, and Ellanicus of Tripolis, were merely known to hate the heresy; and some of them on one pretence or another, some without any, they removed under the authority of royal letters, drove them out of their cities, and appointed others whom they knew to be impious men, to occupy the Churches in their stead.

Case of Marcellus

Of Marcellus , the Bishop of Galatia, it is perhaps superfluous for me to speak; for all men have heard how Eusebius and his fellows, who had been first accused by him of impiety, brought a counter-accusation against him, and caused the old man to be banished. He went up to Rome, and there made his defence, and being required by them, he offered a written declaration of his faith, of which the Council of Sardica approved. But Eusebius and his fellows made no defence, nor, when they were convicted of impiety out of their writings, were they put to shame, but rather assumed greater boldness against all. For they had an introduction to the Emperor from the women , and were formidable to all men.

Martyrdom of Paul of Constantinople

And I suppose no one is ignorant of the case of Paul, Bishop of Constantinople; for the more illustrious any city is, so much the more that which takes place in it is not concealed. A charge was fabricated against him also. For Macedonius his accuser, who has now become Bishop in his stead (I was present myself at the accusation), afterwards held communion with him, and was a Presbyter under Paul himself. And yet when Eusebius with an evil eye wished to seize upon the Bishopric of that city (he had been translated in the same manner from Berytus to Nicomedia), the charge was revived against Paul; and they did not give up their plot, but persisted in the calumny. And he was banished first into Pontus by Constantine, and a second time by Constantius he was sent bound with iron chains to Singara in Mesopotamia, and from thence transferred to Emesa, and a fourth time he was banished to Cucusus in Cappadocia, near the deserts of Mount Taurus; where, as those who were with him have declared, he died by strangulation at their hands. And yet these men who never speak the truth, though guilty of this, were not ashamed after his death to invent another story, representing that he had died from illness; although all who live in that place know the circumstances. And even Philagrius, who was then Deputy-Governor of those parts, and represented all their proceedings in such manner as they desired, was yet astonished at this; and being grieved perhaps that another, and not himself, had done the evil deed, he informed Serapion the Bishop, as well as many other of our friends, that Paul was shut up by them in a very confined and dark place, and left to perish of hunger; and when after six days they went in and found him still alive, they immediately set upon the man, and strangled him. This was the end of his life; and they said that Philip who was Prefect was their agent in the perpetration of this murder. Divine Justice, however, did not overlook this; for not a year passed, when Philip was deprived of his office in great disgrace, so that being reduced to a private station, he became the mockery of those whom he least desired to be the witnesses of his fall. For in extreme distress of mind, groaning and trembling like Cain , and expecting every day that some one would destroy him, far from his country and his friends, he died, like one astounded at his misfortunes, in a manner that he least desired. Moreover these men spare not even after death those against whom they have invented charges while living. They are so eager to show themselves formidable to all, that they banish the living, and show no mercy on the dead; but alone of all the world they manifest their hatred to them that are departed, and conspire against their friends, truly inhuman as they are, and haters of that which is good, savage in temper beyond mere enemies, in behalf of their impiety, who eagerly plot the ruin of me and of all the rest, with no regard to truth, but by false charges.

Restoration of the Catholics

Perceiving this to be the case, the three brothers, Constantine, Constantius, and Constans, caused all after the death of their father to return to their own country and Church; and while they wrote letters concerning the rest to their respective Churches, concerning Athanasius they wrote the following; which likewise shows the violence of the whole proceedings, and proves the murderous disposition of Eusebius and his fellows.

A copy of the Letter of Constantine Cæsar to the people of the Catholic Church in the city of the Alexandrians.

I suppose that it has not escaped the knowledge of your pious minds , etc.

This is his letter; and what more credible witness of their conspiracy could there be than he, who knowing these circumstances has thus written of them?

BOOK II

First Arian Persecution under Constantius

9. Eusebius and his fellows, however, seeing the declension of their heresy, wrote to Rome, as well as to the Emperors Constantine and Constans, to accuse Athanasius: but when the persons who were sent by Athanasius disproved the statements which they had written, they were put to shame by the Emperors; and Julius, Bishop of Rome, wrote to say that a Council ought to be held, wherever we should desire, in order that they might exhibit the charges which they had to make, and might also freely defend themselves concerning those things of which they too were accused. The Presbyters also who were sent by them, when they saw themselves making an exposure, requested that this might be done. Whereupon these men, whose conduct is suspicious in all that they do, when they see that they are not likely to get the better in an Ecclesiastical trial, betake themselves to Constantius alone, and thenceforth bewail themselves, as to the patron of their heresy. 'Spare,' they say, 'the heresy; you see that all men have withdrawn from us; and very few of us are now left. Begin to persecute, for we are being deserted even of

those few, and are left destitute. Those persons whom we forced over to our side, when these men were banished, they now by their return have persuaded again to take part against us. Write letters therefore against them all, and send out Philagrius a second time as Prefect of Egypt, for he is able to carry on a persecution favourably for us, as he has already shown upon trial, and the more so, as he is an apostate. Send also Gregory as Bishop to Alexandria, for he too is able to strengthen our heresy.'

Violent Intrusion of Gregory

Accordingly Constantius at once writes letters, and commences a persecution against all, and sends Philagrius as Prefect with one Arsacius an eunuch; he sends also Gregory with a military force. And the same consequences followed as before. For gathering together a multitude of herdsmen and shepherds, and other dissolute youths belonging to the town, armed with swords and clubs, they attacked in a body the Church which is called the Church of Quirinus ; and some they slew, some they trampled under foot, others they beat with stripes and cast into prison or banished. They haled away many women also, and dragged them openly into the court, and insulted them, dragging them by the hair. Some they proscribed; from some they took away their bread for no other reason, but that they might be induced to join the Arians, and receive Gregory, who had been sent by the Emperor.

The Easterns decline the Council at Rome

Athanasius, however, before these things happened , at the first report of their proceedings, sailed to Rome, knowing the rage of the heretics, and for the purpose of having the Council held as had been determined. And Julius wrote letters to them, and sent the Presbyters Elpidius and Philoxenus, appointing a day , that they might either come, or consider themselves as altogether suspected persons. But as soon as Eusebius and his fellows heard that the trial was to be an Ecclesiastical one, at which no Count would be present, nor soldiers stationed before the doors, and that the proceedings would not be regulated by royal order (for they have always depended upon these things to support them against the Bishops, and without them they have no boldness even to speak); they were so alarmed that they detained the Presbyters till after the appointed time, and pretended an unseemly excuse, that they were not able to come now on account of the war which was begun by the Persians. But this was not the true cause of their delay, but the fears of their own consciences. For what have Bishops to do with war? Or if they were unable on account of the Persians to come to Rome, although it is at a distance and beyond sea, why did they like lions 1 Peter 5:8 go about the parts of the East and those which are near the Persians, seeking who was opposed to them, that they might falsely accuse and banish them?

12. At any rate, when they had dismissed the Presbyters with this improbable excuse, they said to one another, 'Since we are unable to get the advantage in an Ecclesiastical trial, let us exhibit our usual audacity.' Accordingly they write to Philagrius, and cause him after a while to go out with Gregory into Egypt. Whereupon the Bishops are severely scourged and cast into chains. Sarapammon, for instance, Bishop and Confessor, they drive into banishment; Potammon, Bishop and Confessor, who had lost an eye in the persecution, they beat with stripes on the neck so cruelly, that he appeared to be dead before they came to an end. In which condition he was cast aside, and hardly after some hours, being carefully attended and fanned, he revived, God granting him his life; but a short time after he died of the sufferings caused by the stripes, and attained in Christ to the glory of a second martyrdom. And besides these, how many monks were scourged, while Gregory sat by with Balacius the 'Duke!' how many Bishops were wounded! How many virgins were beaten!

Cruelties of Gregory at Alexandria

After this the wretched Gregory called upon all men to have communion with him. But if you demanded of them communion, they were not worthy of stripes: and if you scourged them as if evil persons, why did you ask it of them as if holy? But he had no other end in view, except to fulfil the designs of them that sent him, and to establish the heresy. Wherefore he became in his folly a murderer and an executioner, injurious, crafty, and profane; in one word, an enemy of Christ. He so cruelly persecuted the Bishop's aunt, that even when she died he would not suffer her to be buried. And this would have been her lot; she would have been cast away without burial, had not they who attended on the corpse carried her out as one of their own kindred. Thus even in such things he showed his profane temper. And again when the widows and other mendicants had received alms, he commanded what had been given them to be seized, and the vessels in which they carried their oil and wine to be broken, that he might not only show impiety by robbery, but in his deeds dishonour the Lord; from whom very shortly he will hear those words, 'Inasmuch as you have dishonoured these, you have dishonoured Me. '

Profaneness of Gregory and death of Balacius

And many other things he did, which exceed the power of language to describe, and which whoever should hear would think to be incredible. And the reason why he acted thus was, because he had not received his ordination according to ecclesiastical rule, nor had been called to be a Bishop by tradition ; but had been sent out from court with military power and pomp, as one entrusted with a secular government. Wherefore he boasted rather to be the friend of Governors, than of Bishops and Monks. Whenever, therefore, our Father Antony wrote to him from the mountains, as godliness is an abomination to a sinner, so he abhorred the letters of the holy man. But whenever the Emperor, or a General, or other magistrate, sent him a letter, he was as much overjoyed as those in the Proverbs, of whom the Word has said indignantly, 'Woe unto them who leave the path of uprightness who rejoice to do evil, and delight in the frowardness of the wicked. ' And so he honoured with presents the bearers of these letters; but once when Antony wrote to him he caused Duke Balacius to spit upon the letter, and to cast it from him. But Divine Justice did not overlook this; for no long time after, when the Duke was on horseback, and on his way to the first halt , the horse turned his head, and biting him on the thigh, threw him off; and within three days he died.

BOOK III

Restoration of the Catholics on the Council of Sardica

While they were proceeding in like measures towards all, at Rome about fifty Bishops assembled , and denounced Eusebius and his fellows as persons suspected, afraid to come, and also condemned as unworthy of credit the written statement they had sent; but us they received, and gladly embraced our communion. While these things were taking place, a report of the Council held at Rome, and of the proceedings against the Churches at Alexandria, and through all the East, came to the hearing of the Emperor Constans. He writes to his brother Constantius, and immediately they both determine that a Council shall be called, and matters be brought to a settlement, so that those who had been injured may be released from further suffering, and the injurious be no longer able to perpetrate such outrages. Accordingly there assemble at the city of Sardica both from the East and West to the number of one hundred and seventy Bishops , more or less; those who came from the West were Bishops only, having Hosius for their father, but those from the East brought with them instructors of youth and advocates,

Count Musonianus, and Hesychius the Castrensian; on whose account they came with great alacrity, thinking that everything would be again managed by their authority. For thus by means of these persons they have always shown themselves formidable to any whom they wished to intimidate, and have prosecuted their designs against whomsoever they chose. But when they arrived and saw that the cause was to be conducted as simply an ecclesiastical one, without the interference of the Count or of soldiers; when they saw the accusers who came from every church and city, and the evidence which was brought against them, when they saw the venerable Bishops Arius and Asterius, who came up in their company, withdrawing from them and siding with us, and giving an account of their cunning, and how suspicious their conduct was, and that they were fearing the consequences of a trial, lest they should be convicted by us of being false informers, and it should be discovered by those whom they produced in the character of accusers, that they had themselves suggested all they were to say, and were the contrivers of the plot. Perceiving this to be the case, although they had come with great zeal, as thinking that we should be afraid to meet them, yet now when they saw our alacrity, they shut themselves up in the Palace (for they had their abode there), and proceeded to confer with one another in the following manner: 'We came hither for one result; and we see another; we arrived in company with Counts, and the trial is proceeding without them. We are certainly condemned. You all know the orders that have been given. Athanasius and his fellows have the reports of the proceedings in the Mareotis , by which he is cleared, and we are covered with disgrace. Why then do we delay? Why are we so slow? Let us invent some excuse and be gone, or we shall be condemned if we remain. It is better to suffer the shame of fleeing, than the disgrace of being convicted as false accusers. If we flee, we shall find some means of defending our heresy; and even if they condemn us for our flight, still we have the Emperor as our patron, who will not suffer the people to expel us from the Churches.'

History of the arians ~ Athanasius of Alexandria

Secession of the Easterns at Sardica

Thus then they reasoned with themselves and Hosius and all the other Bishops repeatedly signified to them the alacrity of Athanasius and his fellows, saying, 'They are ready with their defence, and pledge themselves to prove you false accusers.' They said also, 'If you fear the trial, why did you come to meet us? Either you ought not to have come, or now that you have come, not to flee.' When they heard this, being still more alarmed, they had recourse to an excuse even more unseemly than that they pretended at Antioch, viz. that they betook themselves to flight because the Emperor had written to them the news of his victory over the Persians. And this excuse they were not ashamed to send by Eustathius a Presbyter of the Sardican Church. But even thus their flight did not succeed according to their wishes; for immediately the holy Council, of which the great Hosius was president, wrote to them plainly, saying, 'Either come forward and answer the charges which are brought against you, for the false accusations which you have made against others, or know that the Council will condemn you as guilty, and declare Athanasius and his fellows free and clear from all blame.' Whereupon they were rather impelled to flight by the alarms of conscience, than to compliance with the proposals of the letter; for when they saw those who had been injured by them, they did not even turn their faces to listen to their words, but fled with greater speed.

Proceedings of the Council of Sardica

Under these disgraceful and unseemly circumstances their flight took place. And the holy Council, which had been assembled out of more than five and thirty provinces, perceiving the malice of the Arians, admitted Athanasius and his fellows to answer to the charges which the others had brought against them, and to declare the sufferings which they had undergone. And when they had thus made their defence, as we said before, they approved and so highly admired their conduct that they gladly embraced their communion, and wrote letters to all quarters, to the diocese of each, and especially to Alexandria and Egypt, and the Libyas, declaring Athanasius and his friends to be innocent, and free from all blame, and their opponents to be calumniators, evil-doers, and everything rather than Christians. Accordingly they dismissed them in peace; but deposed Stephanus and Menophantus, Acacius and George of Laodicea, Ursacius and Valens, Theodorus and Narcissus. For against Gregory, who had been sent to Alexandria by the Emperor, they put forth a proclamation to the effect that he had never been made a Bishop, and that he ought not to be called a Christian. They therefore declared the ordinations which he professed to have conferred to be void, and commanded that they should not be even named in the Church, on account of their novel and illegal nature. Thus Athanasius and his friends were dismissed in peace (the letters concerning them are inserted at the end on account of their length), and the Council was dissolved.

Arian Persecution after Sardica

But the deposed persons, who ought now to have remained quiet, with those who had separated after so disgraceful a flight, were guilty of such conduct, that their former proceedings appear trifling in comparison of these. For when the people of Adrianople would not have communion with them, as men who had fled from the Council, and had proved culprits, they carried their complaints to the Emperor Constantius, and succeeded in causing ten of the laity to be beheaded, belonging to the Manufactory of arms there, Philagrius, who was there again as Count, assisting their designs in this matter also. The tombs of these persons, which we have seen in passing by, are in front of the city. Then as if they had been quite successful, because they had fled lest they should be convicted of false accusation, they prevailed with the Emperor to command whatsoever they wished to be done. Thus they caused two Presbyters and three Deacons to be banished from Alexandria into Armenia. As to Arius and Asterius, the one Bishop of Petræ in Palestine, the other Bishop in Arabia, who had withdrawn from their party, they not only banished into upper Libya, but also caused them to be treated with insult.

Tyrannical measures against the Alexandrians

And as to Lucius , Bishop of Adrianople, when they saw that he used great boldness of speech against them, and exposed their impiety, they again, as they had done before, caused him to be bound with iron chains on the neck and hands, and so drove him into banishment, where he died, as they know. And Diodorus a Bishop they remove; but against Olympius of Æni, and Theodulus of Trajanople , both Bishops of Thrace, good and orthodox men, when they perceived their hatred of the heresy, they brought false charges. This Eusebius and his fellows had done first of all, and the Emperor Constantius wrote letters on the subject; and next these men revived the accusation. The purport of the letter was, that they should not only be expelled from their cities and churches, but should also suffer capital punishment, wherever they were discovered. However surprising this conduct may be, it is only in accordance with their principles; for as being instructed by Eusebius and his fellows in such proceedings, and as heirs of their impiety and evil principles, they wished to show themselves formidable at Alexandria, as their fathers had done in Thrace. They caused an order to be written, that the ports and gates of the cities should be watched, lest availing themselves of the permission granted by the Council, the banished persons should return to their churches. They also cause orders to be sent to the magistrates at Alexandria, respecting Athanasius and certain Presbyters, named therein, that if either the Bishop , or any of the others, should be found coming to the city or its borders, the magistrate should have power to behead those who were so discovered. Thus this new Jewish heresy does not only deny the Lord, but has also learned to commit murder.

Plot against the Catholic Legates at Antioch

Yet even after this they did not rest; but as the father of their heresy goes about like a lion, seeking whom he may devour, so these obtaining the use of the public posts went about, and whenever they found any that reproached them with their flight, and that hated the Arian heresy, they scourged them, cast them into chains, and caused them to be banished from their country; and they rendered themselves so formidable, as to induce many to dissemble, many to fly into the deserts, rather than willingly even to have any dealings with them. Such were the enormities which their madness prompted them to commit after their flight. Moreover they perpetrate another outrageous act, which is indeed in accordance with the character of their heresy, but is such as we never heard of before, nor is likely soon to take place again, even among the more dissolute of the Gentiles, much less among Christians. The holy Council had sent as Legates the Bishops Vincentius of Capua (this is the Metropolis of Campania), and Euphrates of Agrippina (this is the Metropolis of Upper Gaul), that they might obtain the Emperor's consent to the decision of the Council, that the Bishops should return to their Churches, inasmuch as he was the author of their expulsion. The most religious Constans had also written to his brother , and supported the cause of the Bishops. But these admirable men, who are equal to any act of audacity, when they saw the two Legates at Antioch, consulted together and formed a plot, which Stephanus undertook by himself to execute, as being a suitable instrument for such purposes. Accordingly they hire a common harlot, even at the season of the most holy Easter, and stripping her introduce her by night into the apartment of the Bishop Euphrates. The harlot who thought that it was a young man who had sent to invite her, at first willingly accompanied them; but when they thrust her in, and she saw the man asleep and unconscious of what was going on, and when presently she distinguished his features, and beheld the face of an old man, and the array of a Bishop, she immediately cried aloud, and declared that violence was used towards her. They desired her to be silent, and to lay a false charge against the Bishop; and so when it was day, the matter was noised abroad, and all the city ran together; and those who came from the Palace were in great commotion, wondering at the report which had been spread abroad, and demanding that it should not be passed by in silence. An enquiry, therefore, was made, and her master gave information concerning those who came to fetch the harlot, and these informed against Stephanus; for they were his Clergy. Stephanus, therefore, is deposed , and Leontius the eunuch appointed in his place, only that the Arian heresy may not want a supporter.

Constantius' change of mind

And now the Emperor Constantius, feeling some compunctions, returned to himself; and concluding from their conduct towards Euphrates, that their attacks upon the others were of the same kind, he gives orders that the Presbyters and Deacons who had been banished from Alexandria into Armenia should immediately be released. He also writes publicly to Alexandria , commanding that the clergy and laity who were friends of Athanasius should suffer no further persecution. And when Gregory died about ten months after, he sends for Athanasius with every mark of honour, writing to him no less than three times a very friendly letter in which he exhorted him to take courage and come. He sends also a Presbyter and a Deacon, that he may be still further encouraged to return; for he thought that, through alarm at what had taken place before, I did not care to return. Moreover he writes to his brother Constans, that he also would exhort me to return. And he affirmed that he had been expecting Athanasius a whole year, and that he would not permit any change to be made, or any ordination to take place, as he was preserving the Churches for Athanasius their Bishop.

Athanasius visits Constantius

When therefore he wrote in this strain, and encouraged him by means of many (for he caused Polemius, Datianus, Bardion, Thalassus , Taurus , and Florentius, his Counts, in whom Athanasius could best confide, to write also): Athanasius committing the whole matter to God, who had stirred the conscience of Constantius to do this, came with his friends to him; and he gave him a favourable audience , and sent him away to go to his country and his Churches, writing at the same time to the magistrates in the several places, that whereas he had before commanded the ways to be guarded, they should now grant him a free passage. Then when the Bishop complained of the sufferings he had undergone, and of the letters which the Emperor had written against him, and besought him that the false accusations against him might not be revived by his enemies after his departure, saying , 'If you please, summon these persons; for as far as we are concerned they are at liberty to stand forth, and we will expose their conduct;' he would not do this, but commanded that whatever had been before slanderously written against him should all be destroyed and obliterated, affirming that he would never again listen to any such accusations, and that his purpose was fixed and unalterable. This he did not simply say, but sealed his words with oaths, calling upon God to be witness of them. And so encouraging him with many other words, and desiring him to be of good courage, he sends the following letters to the Bishops and Magistrates.

Constantius Augustus, the Great, the Conqueror, to the Bishops and Clergy of the Catholic Church.

The most Reverend Athanasius has not been deserted by the grace of God , etc.

Another Letter.

From Constantius to the people of Alexandria.

Desiring as we do your welfare in all respects , etc.

Another Letter.

Constantius Augustus, the Conqueror, to Nestorius, Prefect of Egypt.

It is well known that an order was heretofore given by us, and that certain documents are to be found prejudicial to the estimation of the most reverend Bishop Athanasius; and that these exist among the Orders of your worship. Now we desire your Sobriety, of which we have good proof, to transmit to our Court, in compliance with this our order, all the letters respecting the fore-mentioned person, which are found in your Order-book.

The following is the letter which he wrote after the death of the blessed Constans. It was written in Latin, and is here translated into Greek.

Constantius Augustus, the Conqueror, to Athanasius.

It is not unknown to your Prudence, that it was my constant prayer, that prosperity might attend my late brother Constans in all his undertakings; and your wisdom may therefore imagine how greatly I was afflicted when I learned that he had been taken off by most unhallowed hands. Now whereas there are certain persons who at the present truly mournful time are endeavouring to alarm you, I have therefore thought it right to address this letter to your Constancy, to exhort you that, as becomes a Bishop, you would teach the people those things which pertain to the divine religion, and that, as you are accustomed to do, you would employ your time in prayers together with them, and not give credit to vain rumours, whatever they may be. For our fixed determination is, that you should continue, agreeably to our desire, to perform the office of a Bishop in your own place. May Divine Providence preserve you, most beloved parent, many years.

History of the arians ~ Athanasius of Alexandria

Return of Athanasius from second exile

Under these circumstances, when they had at length taken their leave, and begun their journey, those who were friendly rejoiced to see a friend; but of the other party, some were confounded at the sight of him; others not having the confidence to appear, hid themselves; and others repented of what they had written against the Bishop. Thus all the Bishops of Palestine , except some two or three, and those men of suspected character, so willingly received Athanasius, and embraced communion with him, that they wrote to excuse themselves, on the ground that in what they had formerly written, they had acted, not according to their own wishes, but by compulsion. Of the Bishops of Egypt and the Libyan provinces, of the laity both of those countries and of Alexandria, it is superfluous for me to speak. They all ran together, and were possessed with unspeakable delight, that they had not only received their friends alive contrary to their hopes; but that they were also delivered from the heretics who were as tyrants and as raging dogs towards them. Accordingly great was their joy , the people in the congregations encouraging one another in virtue. How many unmarried women, who were before ready to enter upon marriage, now remained virgins to Christ! How many young men, seeing the examples of others, embraced the monastic life! How many fathers persuaded their children, and how many were urged by their children, not to be hindered from Christian asceticism! How many wives persuaded their husbands, and how many were persuaded by their husbands, to give themselves to prayer 1 Corinthians 7:5, as the Apostle has spoken! How many widows and how many orphans, who were before hungry and naked, now through the great zeal of the people, were no longer hungry, and went forth clothed! In a word, so great was their emulation in virtue, that you would have thought every family and every house a Church, by reason of the goodness of its inmates, and the prayers which were offered to God. And in the Churches there was a profound and wonderful peace, while the Bishops wrote from all quarters, and received from Athanasius the customary letters of peace.

Recantation of Ursacius and Valens

Moreover Ursacius and Valens, as if suffering the scourge of conscience, came to another mind, and wrote to the Bishop himself a friendly and peaceable letter , although they had received no communication from him. And going up to Rome they repented, and confessed that all their proceedings and assertions against him were founded in falsehood and mere calumny. And they not only voluntarily did this, but also anathematized the Arian heresy, and presented a written declaration of their repentance, addressing to the Bishop Julius the following letter in Latin, which has been translated into Greek. The copy was sent to us in Latin by Paul , Bishop of Treveri.

Translation from the Latin.

Ursacius and Valens to my Lord the most blessed Pope Julius.

Whereas it is well known that we , etc.

Translation from the Latin.

The Bishops Ursacius and Valens to my Lord and Brother, the Bishop Athanasius.

Having an opportunity of sending , etc.

After writing these, they also subscribed the letters of peace which were presented to them by Peter and

Irenæus, Presbyters of Athanasius, and by Ammonius a layman, who were passing that way, although Athanasius had sent no communication to them even by these persons.

Triumph of Athanasius

Now who was not filled with admiration at witnessing these things, and the great peace that prevailed in the Churches? Who did not rejoice to see the concord of so many Bishops? Who did not glorify the Lord, beholding the delight of the people in their assemblies? How many enemies repented! How many excused themselves who had formerly accused him falsely! How many who formerly hated him, now showed affection for him! How many of those who had written against him, recanted their assertions? Many also who had sided with the Arians, not through choice but by necessity, came by night and excused themselves. They anathematized the heresy, and besought him to pardon them, because, although through the plots and calumnies of these men they appeared bodily on their side, yet in their hearts they held communion with Athanasius, and were always with him. Believe me, this is true.

BOOK IV

Second ArianPersecution under Constantius

But the inheritors of the opinions and impiety of Eusebius and his fellows, the eunuch Leontius , who ought not to remain in communion even as a layman , because he mutilated himself that he might henceforward be at liberty to sleep with one Eustolium, who is a wife as far as he is concerned, but is called a virgin; and George and Acacius, and Theodorus, and Narcissus, who are deposed by the Council; when they heard and saw these things, were greatly ashamed. And when they perceived the unanimity and peace that existed between Athanasius and the Bishops (they were more than four hundred , from great Rome, and all Italy, from Calabria, Apulia, Campania, Bruttia, Sicily, Sardinia, Corsica, and the whole of Africa; and those from Gaul, Britain, and Spain, with the great Confessor Hosius; and also those from Pannonia, Noricum, Siscia, Dalmatia, Dardania, Dacia, Mœsia, Macedonia, Thessaly, and all Achaia, and from Crete, Cyprus, and Lycia, with most of those from Palestine, Isauria, Egypt, the Thebais, the whole of Libya, and Pentapolis); when I say they perceived these things, they were possessed with envy and fear; with envy, on account of the communion of so many together; and with fear, lest those who had been entrapped by them should be brought over by the unanimity of so great a number, and henceforth their heresy should be triumphantly exposed, and everywhere proscribed.

Relapse of Ursacius and Valens

First of all they persuade Ursacius, Valens and their fellows to change sides again, and like dogs to return to their own vomit, and like swine to wallow again in the former mire of their impiety; and they make this excuse for their retractation, that they did it through fear of the most religious Constans. And yet even had there been cause for fear, yet if they had confidence in what they had done, they ought not to have become traitors to their friends. But when there was no cause for fear, and yet they were guilty of a lie, are they not deserving of utter condemnation? For no soldier was present, no Palatine or Notary had been sent, as they now send them, nor yet was the Emperor there, nor had they been invited by any one, when they wrote their recantation. But they voluntarily went up to Rome, and of their own accord recanted and wrote it down in the Church, where there was no fear from without, where the only fear is the fear of God, and where every one has liberty of conscience. And yet although they have a second time become Arians, and then have devised this unseemly excuse for their conduct, they are still without shame.

History of the arians ~ Athanasius of Alexandria

Constantius changes sides again

In the next place they went in a body to the Emperor Constantius, and besought him, saying, 'When we first made our request to you, we were not believed; for we told you, when you sent for Athanasius, that by inviting him to come forward, you are expelling our heresy. For he has been opposed to it from the very first, and never ceases to anathematize it. He has already written letters against us into all parts of the world, and the majority of men have embraced communion with him; and even of those who seemed to be on our side, some have been gained over by him, and others are likely to be. And we are left alone, so that the fear is, lest the character of our heresy become known, and henceforth both we and you gain the name of heretics. And if this come to pass, you must take care that we be not classed with the Manichæans. Therefore begin again to persecute, and support the heresy, for it accounts you its king.' Such was the language of their iniquity. And the Emperor, when in his passage through the country on his hasty march against Magnentius , he saw the communion of the Bishops with Athanasius, like one set on fire, suddenly changed his mind, and no longer remembered his oaths, but was alike forgetful of what he had written and regardless of the duty he owed his brother. For in his letters to him, as well as in his interview with Athanasius, he took oaths that he

63

would not act otherwise than as the people should wish, and as should be agreeable to the Bishops. But his zeal for impiety caused him at once to forget all these things. And yet one ought not to wonder that after so many letters and so many oaths Constantius had altered his mind, when we remember that Pharaoh of old, the tyrant of Egypt, after frequently promising and by that means obtaining a remission of his punishments, likewise changed, until he at last perished together with his associates.

Constantius begins to persecute

He compelled then the people in every city to change their party; and on arriving at Arles and Milan , he proceeded to act entirely in accordance with the designs and suggestions of the heretics; or rather they acted themselves, and receiving authority from him, furiously attacked every one. Letters and orders were immediately sent hither to the Prefect, that for the future the grain should be taken from Athanasius and given to those who favoured the Arian doctrines, and that whoever pleased might freely insult them that held communion with him; and the magistrates were threatened if they did not hold communion with the Arians. These things were but the prelude to what afterwards took place under the direction of the Duke Syrianus. Orders were sent also to the more distant parts, and Notaries dispatched to every city, and Palatines, with threats to the Bishops and Magistrates, directing the Magistrates to urge on the Bishops, and informing the Bishops that either they must subscribe against Athanasius, and hold communion with the Arians, or themselves undergo the punishment of exile, while the people who took part with them were to understand that chains, and insults, and scourgings, and the loss of their possessions, would be their portion. These orders were not neglected, for the commissioners had in their company the Clergy of Ursacius and Valens, to inspire them with zeal, and to inform the Emperor if the Magistrates neglected their duty. The other heresies, as younger sisters of their own , they permitted to blaspheme the Lord, and only conspired against the Christians, not enduring to hear orthodox language concerning Christ. How many Bishops in consequence, according to the words of Scripture, were brought before rulers and kings Mark 13:9, and received this sentence from magistrates, 'Subscribe, or withdraw from your churches, for the Emperor has commanded you to be deposed!' How many in every city were roughly handled, lest they should accuse them as friends of the Bishops! Moreover letters were sent to the city authorities, and a threat of a fine was held out to them, if they did not compel the Bishops of their respective cities to subscribe. In short, every place and every city was full of fear and confusion, while the Bishops were dragged along to trial, and the magistrates witnessed the lamentations and groans of the people.

Persecution by Constantius

Such were the proceedings of the Palatine commissioners; on the other hand, those admirable persons, confident in the patronage which they had obtained, display great zeal, and cause some of the Bishops to be summoned before the Emperor, while they persecute others by letters, inventing charges against them; to the intent that the one might be overawed by the presence of Constantius, and the other, through fear of the commissioners and the threats held out to them in these pretended accusations, might be brought to renounce their orthodox and pious opinions. In this manner it was that the Emperor forced so great a multitude of Bishops, partly by threats, and partly by promises, to declare, 'We will no longer hold communion with Athanasius.' For those who came for an interview, were not admitted to his presence, nor allowed any relaxation, not so much as to go out of their dwellings, until they had either subscribed, or refused and incurred banishment thereupon. And this he did because he saw that the heresy was hateful to all men. For this reason especially he compelled so many to add their names to the small number of the Arians, his earnest desire being to collect together a crowd of names, both from envy of the Bishop, and for the sake of making a show in favour of the Arian impiety, of which he is the patron; supposing that he will be able to alter the truth, as easily as he can influence the minds of men. He knows not, nor has ever read, how that the Sadducees and the Herodians, taking unto them the Pharisees, were not able to obscure the truth; rather it shines out thereby more brightly every day, while they crying out, 'We have no king but Cæsar ,' and obtaining the judgment of Pilate in their favour, are nevertheless left destitute, and wait in utter shame, expecting shortly to become bereft, like the partridge , when they shall see their patron near his death.

History of the arians ~ Athanasius of Alexandria

Persecution is from the Devil

Now if it was altogether unseemly in any of the Bishops to change their opinions merely from fear of these things, yet it was much more so, and not the part of men who have confidence in what they believe, to force and compel the unwilling. In this manner it is that the Devil, when he has no truth on his side, attacks and breaks down the doors of them that admit him with axes and hammers. But our Saviour is so gentle that He teaches thus, 'If any man wills to come after Me,' and, 'Whoever wills to be My disciple Matthew 16:24;' and coming to each He does not force them, but knocks at the door and says, 'Open unto Me, My sister, My spouse Song of Songs 5:2;' and if they open to Him, He enters in, but if they delay and will not, He departs from them. For the truth is not preached with swords or with darts, nor by means of soldiers; but by persuasion and counsel. But what persuasion is there where fear of the Emperor prevails? Or what counsel is there, when he who withstands them receives at last banishment and death? Even David, although he was a king, and had his enemy in his power, prevented not the soldiers by an exercise of authority when they wished to kill his enemy, but, as the Scripture says, David persuaded his men by arguments, and suffered them not to rise up and put Saul to death. 1 Samuel 26:9 But he, being without arguments of reason, forces all men by his power, that it may be shown to all, that their wisdom is not according to God, but merely human, and that they who favour the Arian doctrines have indeed no king but Cæsar; for by his means it is that these enemies of Christ accomplish whatsoever they wish to do. But while they thought that they were carrying on their designs against many by his means, they knew not that they were making many to be confessors, of whom are those who have lately made so glorious a confession, religious men, and excellent Bishops, Paulinus Bishop of Treveri, the metropolis of the Gauls, Lucifer, Bishop of the metropolis of Sardinia, Eusebius of Vercelli in Italy, and Dionysius of Milan, which is the metropolis of Italy. These the Emperor summoned before him, and commanded them to subscribe against Athanasius, and to hold communion with the heretics; and when they were astonished at this novel procedure, and said that there was no Ecclesiastical Canon to this effect, he immediately said, 'Whatever I will, be that esteemed a Canon; the Bishops of Syria let me thus speak. Either then obey, or go into banishment.'

Banishment of the Western Bishops spread the knowledge of the truth

When the Bishops heard this they were utterly amazed, and stretching forth their hands to God, they used great boldness of speech against him teaching him that the kingdom was not his, but God's, who had given it to him, Whom also they bid him fear, lest He should suddenly take it away from him. And they threatened him with the day of judgment, and warned him against infringing Ecclesiastical order, and mingling Roman sovereignty with the constitution of the Church, and against introducing the Arian heresy into the Church of God. But he would not listen to them, nor permit them to speak further, but threatened them so much the more, and drew his sword against them, and gave orders for some of them to be led to execution; although afterwards, like Pharaoh, he repented. The holy men therefore shaking off the dust, and looking up to God, neither feared the threats of the Emperor, nor betrayed their cause before his drawn sword; but received their banishment, as a service pertaining to their ministry. And as they passed along, they preached the Gospel in every place and city , although they were in bonds, proclaiming the orthodox faith, anathematizing the Arian heresy, and stigmatizing the recantation of Ursacius and Valens. But this was contrary to the intention of their enemies; for the greater was the distance of their place of banishment, so much the more was the hatred against them increased, while the wanderings of these men were but the heralding of their impiety. For who that saw them as they passed along, did not greatly admire them as Confessors, and renounce and abominate the others, calling them not only impious men, but executioners and murderers, and everything rather than Christians?

BOOK V

Persecution and Lapse of Liberius

35. Now it had been better if from the first Constantius had never become connected with this heresy at all; or being connected with it, if he had not yielded so much to those impious men; or having yielded to them, if he had stood by them only thus far, so that judgment might come upon them all for these atrocities alone. But as it would seem, like madmen, having fixed themselves in the bonds of impiety, they are drawing down upon their own heads a more severe judgment. Thus from the first they spared not even Liberius, Bishop of Rome, but extended their fury even to those parts; they respected not his bishopric, because it was an Apostolical throne; they felt no reverence for Rome, because she is the Metropolis of Romania ; they remembered not that formerly in their letters they had spoken of her Bishops as Apostolical men. But confounding all things together, they at once forgot everything, and cared only to show their zeal in behalf of impiety. When they perceived that he was an orthodox man and hated the Arian heresy, and earnestly endeavoured to persuade all persons to renounce and withdraw from it, these impious men reasoned thus

with themselves: 'If we can persuade Liberius, we shall soon prevail over all.' Accordingly they accused him falsely before the Emperor; and he, expecting easily to draw over all men to his side by means of Liberius, writes to him, and sends a certain eunuch called Eusebius with letters and offerings, to cajole him with the presents, and to threaten him with the letters. The eunuch accordingly went to Rome, and first proposed to Liberius to subscribe against Athanasius, and to hold communion with the Arians, saying, 'The Emperor wishes it, and commands you to do so.' And then showing him the offerings, he took him by the hand, and again besought him saying, 'Obey the Emperor, and receive these.'

The Eunuch Eusebius attempts Liberius in vain

But the Bishop endeavoured to convince him, reasoning with him thus: 'How is it possible for me to do this against Athanasius? How can we condemn a man, whom not one Council only, but a second assembled from all parts of the world, has fairly acquitted, and whom the Church of the Romans dismissed in peace? Who will approve of our conduct, if we reject in his absence one, whose presence among us we gladly welcomed, and admitted him to our communion? This is no Ecclesiastical Canon; nor have we had transmitted to us any such tradition from the Fathers, who in their turn received from the great and blessed Apostle Peter. But if the Emperor is really concerned for the peace of the Church, if he requires our letters respecting Athanasius to be reversed, let their proceedings both against him and against all the others be reversed also; and then let an Ecclesiastical Council be called at a distance from the Court, at which the Emperor shall not be present, nor any Count be admitted, nor magistrate to threaten us, but where only the fear of God and the Apostolical rule shall prevail; that so in the first place, the faith of the Church may be secure, as the Fathers defined it in the Council of Nicæa, and the supporters of the Arian doctrines may be cast out, and their heresy anathematized. And then after that, an enquiry being made into the charges brought against Athanasius, and any other besides, as well as into those things of which the other party is accused, let the culprits be cast out, and the innocent receive encouragement and support. For it is impossible that they who maintain an impious creed can be admitted as members of a Council: nor is it fit that an enquiry into matters of conduct should precede the enquiry concerning the faith ; but all diversity of opinions on points of faith ought first to be eradicated, and then the enquiry made into matters of conduct. Our Lord Jesus Christ did not heal them that were afflicted, until they showed and declared what faith they had in Him. These things we have received from the Fathers; these report to the Emperor; for they are both profitable for him and edifying to the Church. But let not Ursacius and Valens be listened to, for they have retracted their former assertions, and in what they now say they are not to be trusted.'

History of the arians ~ Athanasius of Alexandria

Liberius refuses the Emperor's offering

These were the words of the Bishop Liberius. And the eunuch, who was vexed, not so much because he would not subscribe, as because he found him an enemy to the heresy, forgetting that he was in the presence of a Bishop, after threatening him severely, went away with the offerings; and next commits an offense, which is foreign to a Christian, and too audacious for a eunuch. In imitation of the transgression of Saul, he went to the Martyry of the Apostle Peter, and then presented the offerings. But Liberius having notice of it, was very angry with the person who kept the place, that he had not prevented him, and cast out the offerings as an unlawful sacrifice, which increased the anger of the mutilated creature against him. Consequently he exasperates the Emperor against him, saying, 'The matter that concerns us is no longer the obtaining the subscription of Liberius, but the fact that he is so resolutely opposed to the heresy, that he anathematizes the Arians by name.' He also stirs up the other eunuchs to say the same; for many of those who were about Constantius, or rather the whole number of them, are eunuchs, who engross all the influence with him, and it is impossible to do anything there without them. The Emperor accordingly writes to Rome, and again Palatines, and Notaries, and Counts are sent off with letters to the Prefect, in order that either they may inveigle Liberius by stratagem away from Rome and send him to the Court to him, or else persecute him by violence.

The evil influence of Eunuchs at Court

Such being the tenor of the letters, there also fear and treachery immediately became rife throughout the whole city. How many were the families against which threats were held out! How many received great promises on condition of their acting against Liberius! How many Bishops hid themselves when they saw these things! How many noble women retired to country places in consequence of the calumnies of the enemies of Christ! How many ascetics were made the objects of their plots! How many who were sojourning there, and had made that place their home, did they cause to be persecuted! How often and how strictly did they guard the harbour and the approaches to the gates, lest any orthodox person should enter and visit Liberius! Rome also had trial of the enemies of Christ, and now experienced what before she would not believe, when she heard how the other Churches in every city were ravaged by them. It was the eunuchs who instigated these proceedings against all. And the most remarkable circumstance in the matter is this; that the Arian heresy which denies the Son of God, receives its support from eunuchs, who, as both their bodies are fruitless, and their souls barren of virtue, cannot bear even to hear the name of son. The Eunuch of Ethiopia indeed, though he understood not what he read Acts 8:27, believed the words of Philip, when he taught him concerning the Saviour; but the eunuchs of Constantius cannot endure the confession of Peter , nay, they turn away when the Father manifests the Son, and madly rage against those who say, that the Son of God is His genuine Son, thus claiming as a heresy of eunuchs, that there is no genuine and true offspring of the Father. On these grounds it is that the law forbids such persons to be admitted into any ecclesiastical Council ; notwithstanding which they have now regarded these as competent judges of ecclesiastical causes, and whatever seems good to them, that Constantius decrees, while men with the name of Bishops dissemble with them. Oh! Who shall be their historian? Who shall transmit the record of these things to another generation? Who indeed would believe it, were he to hear it, that eunuchs who are scarcely entrusted with household services (for theirs is a pleasure-loving race, that has no serious concern but that of hindering in others what nature has taken from them); that these, I say, now exercise authority in ecclesiastical matters, and that Constantius in submission to their will treacherously conspired against all, and banished Liberius!

History of the arians ~ Athanasius of Alexandria

Liberius's speech to Constantius

For after the Emperor had frequently written to Rome, had threatened, sent commissioners, devised schemes, on the persecution subsequently breaking out at Alexandria, Liberius is dragged before him, and uses great boldness of speech towards him. 'Cease,' he said, 'to persecute the Christians; attempt not by my means to introduce impiety into the Church. We are ready to suffer anything rather than to be called Arian madmen. We are Christians; compel us not to become enemies of Christ. We also give you this counsel: fight not against Him who gave you this empire, nor show impiety towards Him instead of thankfulness ;' persecute not them that believe in Him, lest you also hear the words, 'It is hard for you to kick against the pricks Acts 9:5.' Nay, I would that you might hear them, that you might obey, as the holy Paul did. Behold, here we are; we have come, before they fabricate charges. For this cause we hastened hither, knowing that banishment awaits us at your hands, that we might suffer before a charge encounters us, and that all may clearly see that all the others too have suffered as we shall suffer, and that the charges brought against them were fabrications of their enemies, and all their proceedings were mere calumny and falsehood.'

Banishment of Liberius and others

These were the words of Liberius at that time, and he was admired by all men for them. But the Emperor instead of answering , only gave orders for their banishment, separating each of them from the rest, as he had done in the former cases. For he had himself devised this plan in the banishments which he inflicted, that so the severity of his punishments might be greater than that of former tyrants and persecutors. In the former persecution Maximian, who was then Emperor, commanded a number of Confessors to be banished together , and thus lightened their punishment by the consolation which he gave them in each other's society. But this man was more savage than he; he separated those who had spoken boldly and confessed together, he put asunder those who were united by the bond of faith, that when they came to die they might not see one another; thinking that bodily separation can disunite also the affections of the mind, and that being severed from each other, they would forget the concord and unanimity which existed among them. He knew not that however each one may remain apart from the rest, he has nevertheless with him that Lord, whom they confessed in one body together, who will also provide (as he did in the case of the Prophet Elisha 2 Kings 6:16) that more shall be with each of them, than there are soldiers with Constantius. Of a truth iniquity is blind; for in that they thought to afflict the Confessors, by separating them from one another, they rather brought thereby a great injury upon themselves. For had they continued in each other's company, and abode together, the pollutions of those impious men would have been proclaimed from one place only; but now by putting them asunder, they have made their impious heresy and wickedness to spread abroad and become known in every place.

Lapse of Liberius

Who that shall hear what they did in the course of these proceedings will not think them to be anything rather than Christians? When Liberius sent Eutropius, a Presbyter, and Hilarius, a Deacon, with letters to the Emperor, at the time that Lucifer and his fellows made their confession, they banished the Presbyter on the spot, and after stripping Hilarius the Deacon and scourging him on the back, they banished him too, clamouring at him, 'Why did you not resist Liberius instead of being the bearer of letters from him.' Ursacius and Valens, with the eunuchs who sided with them, were the authors of this outrage. The Deacon, while he was being scourged, praised the Lord, remembering His words, 'I gave My back to the smiters Isaiah 50:6;' but they while they scourged him laughed and mocked him, feeling no shame that they were insulting a Levite. Indeed they acted but consistently in laughing while he continued to praise God; for it is the part of Christians to endure stripes, but to scourge Christians is the outrage of a Pilate or a Caiaphas. Thus they endeavoured at the first to corrupt the Church of the Romans, wishing to introduce impiety into it as well as others. But Liberius after he had been in banishment two years gave way, and from fear of threatened death subscribed. Yet even this only shows their violent conduct, and the hatred of Liberius against the heresy, and his support of Athanasius, so long as he was suffered to exercise a free choice. For that which men are forced by torture to do contrary to their first judgment, ought not to be considered the willing deed of those who are in fear, but rather of their tormentors. They however attempted everything in support of their heresy, while the people in every Church, preserving the faith which they had learned, waited for the return of their teachers, and condemned the Antichristian heresy, and all avoid it, as they would a serpent.

BOOK VI

Persecution and Lapse of Hosius

But although they had done all this, yet these impious men thought they had accomplished nothing, so long as the great Hosius escaped their wicked machinations. And now they undertook to extend their fury to that great old man. They felt no shame at the thought that he is the father of the Bishops; they regarded not that he had been a Confessor ; they reverenced not the length of his Episcopate, in which he had continued more than sixty years; but they set aside everything, and looked only to the interests of their heresy, as being of a truth such as neither fear God, nor regard man. Luke 18:2 Accordingly they went to Constantius, and again employed such arguments as the following: 'We have done everything; we have banished the Bishop of the Romans; and before him a very great number of other Bishops, and have filled every place with alarm. But these strong measures of yours are as nothing to us, nor is our success at all more secure, so long as Hosius remains. While he is in his own place, the rest also continue in their Churches, for he is able by his arguments and his faith to persuade all men against us. He is the president of Councils , and his letters are everywhere attended to. He it was who put forth the Nicene Confession, and proclaimed everywhere that the Arians were heretics. If therefore he is suffered to remain, the banishment of the rest is of no avail, for our heresy will be destroyed. Begin then to persecute him also and spare him not, ancient as he is. Our heresy knows not to honour even the hoary hairs of the aged.'

Brave resistance of Hosius

Upon hearing this, the Emperor no longer delayed, but knowing the man, and the dignity of his years, wrote to summon him. This was when he first began his attempt upon Liberius. Upon his arrival he desired him, and urged him with the usual arguments, with which he thought also to deceive the others, that he would subscribe against us, and hold communion with the Arians. But the old man, scarcely bearing to hear the words, and grieved that he had even ventured to utter such a proposal, severely rebuked him, and after gaining his consent, withdrew to his own country and Church. But the heretics still complaining, and instigating him to proceed (he had the eunuchs also to remind him and to urge him further), the Emperor again wrote in threatening terms; but still Hosius, while he endured their insults, was unmoved by any fear of their designs against him, and remaining firm to his purpose, as one who had built the house of his faith upon the rock, he spoke boldly against the heresy, regarding the threats held out to him in the letters but as drops of rain and blasts of wind. And although Constantius wrote frequently, sometimes flattering him with the title of Father, and sometimes threatening and recounting the names of those who had been banished, and saying, 'Will you continue the only person to oppose the heresy? Be persuaded and subscribe against

Athanasius; for whoever subscribes against him thereby embraces with us the Arian cause;' still Hosius remained fearless, and while suffering these insults, wrote an answer in such terms as these. We have read the letter, which is placed at the end.

'Hosius to Constantius the Emperor sends health in the Lord.'

I was a Confessor at the first, when a persecution arose in the time of your grandfather Maximian; and if you shall persecute me, I am ready now, too, to endure anything rather than to shed innocent blood and to betray the truth. But I cannot approve of your conduct in writing after this threatening manner. Cease to write thus; adopt not the cause of Arius, nor listen to those in the East, nor give credit to Ursacius, Valens and their fellows. For whatever they assert, it is not on account of Athanasius, but for the sake of their own heresy. Believe my statement, O Constantius, who am of an age to be your grandfather. I was present at the Council of Sardica, when you and your brother Constans of blessed memory assembled us all together; and on my own account I challenged the enemies of Athanasius, when they came to the church where I abode , that if they had anything against him they might declare it; desiring them to have confidence, and not to expect otherwise than that a right judgment would be passed in all things. This I did once and again, requesting them, if they were unwilling to appear before the whole Council, yet to appear before me alone; promising them also, that if he should be proved guilty, he should certainly be rejected by us; but if he should be found to be blameless, and should prove them to be calumniators, that if they should then refuse to hold communion with him, I would persuade him to go with me into the Spains. Athanasius was willing to comply with these conditions, and made no objection to my proposal; but they, altogether distrusting their cause, would not consent. And on another occasion Athanasius came to your Court, when you wrote for him, and his enemies being at the time in Antioch, he requested that they might be summoned either altogether or separately, in order that they might either convict him, or be convicted, and might either in his presence prove him to be what they represented, or cease to accuse him when absent. To this proposal also you would not listen, and they equally rejected it. Why then do you still give ear to them that speak evil of him? How can you endure Valens and Ursacius, although they have retracted and made a written confession of their calumnies? For it is not true, as they pretend, that they were forced to confess; there were no soldiers at hand to influence them; your brother was not cognizant of the matter. No, such things were not done under his government, as are done now; God forbid. But they voluntarily went up to Rome, and in the presence of the Bishop and Presbyters wrote their recantation, having previously addressed to Athanasius a friendly and peaceable letter. And if they pretend that force was employed towards them, and acknowledge that this is an evil thing, which you also disapprove of; then do you cease to use force; write no letters, send no Counts; but release those that have been banished, lest while you are complaining of violence, they do but exercise greater violence. When was any such thing done by Constans? What Bishop suffered banishment? When did he appear as arbiter of an Ecclesiastical trial? When did any Palatine of his compel men to subscribe against any one, that Valens and his fellows should be able to affirm this? Cease these proceedings, I beseech you, and remember that you are a mortal man. Be afraid of the day of judgment, and keep yourself pure thereunto. Intrude not yourself into Ecclesiastical matters, neither give commands unto us concerning them; but learn them from us. God has put into your hands the kingdom; to us He has entrusted the affairs of His Church; and as he who would steal the empire from you would resist the ordinance of God, so likewise fear on your part lest by taking upon yourself the government of the Church, you become guilty of a great offense. It is written, Render unto Cæsar the things that are Cæsar's, and unto God the things that are God's Matthew 22:21 . Neither therefore is it permitted unto us to exercise an earthly rule, nor have you, Sire, any authority to burn incense. These things I write unto you out of a concern for your salvation. With regard to the subject of your letters, this is my determination; I will not unite myself to the Arians; I anathematize their heresy. Neither will I subscribe against Athanasius, whom both we and the Church of the

History of the arians ~ Athanasius of Alexandria

Romans and the whole Council pronounced to be guiltless. And yourself also, when you understood this, sent for the man, and gave him permission to return with honour to his country and his Church. What reason then can there be for so great a change in your conduct? The same persons who were his enemies before, are so now also; and the things they now whisper to his prejudice (for they do not declare them openly in his presence), the same they spoke against him, before you sent for him; the same they spread abroad concerning him when they come to the Council. And when I required them to come forward, as I have before said, they were unable to produce their proofs; had they possessed any, they would not have fled so disgracefully. Who then persuaded you so long after to forget your own letters and declarations? Forbear, and be not influenced by evil men, lest while you act for the mutual advantage of yourself and them, you render yourself responsible. For here you comply with their desires, hereafter in the judgment you will have to answer for doing so alone. These men desire by your means to injure their enemy, and wish to make you the minister of their wickedness, in order that through your help they may sow the seeds of their accursed heresy in the Church. Now it is not a prudent thing to cast one's self into manifest danger for the pleasure of others. Cease then, I beseech you, O Constantius, and be persuaded by me. These things it becomes me to write, and you not to despise.'

Lapse of Hosius, due to cruel persecution

Such were the sentiments, and such the letter, of the Abraham-like old man, Hosius, truly so called. But the Emperor desisted not from his designs, nor ceased to seek an occasion against him; but continued to threaten him severely, with a view either to bring him over by force, or to banish him if he refused to comply. And as the Officers and Satraps of Babylon Daniel 6:5, seeking an occasion against Daniel, found none except in the law of his God; so likewise these present Satraps of impiety were unable to invent any charge against the old man (for this true Hosius, and his blameless life were known to all), except the charge of hatred to their heresy. They therefore proceeded to accuse him; though not under the same circumstances as those others accused Daniel to Darius, for Darius was grieved to hear the charge, but as Jezebel accused Naboth, and as the Jews applied themselves to Herod. And they said, 'He not only will not subscribe against Athanasius, but also on his account condemns us; and his hatred to the heresy is so great, that he also writes to others, that they should rather suffer death, than become traitors to the truth. For, he says, our beloved Athanasius also is persecuted for the Truth's sake, and Liberius, Bishop of Rome, and all the rest, are treacherously assailed.'

When this patron of impiety, and Emperor of heresy, Constantius, heard this, and especially that there were others also in the Spains of the same mind as Hosius, after he had tempted them also to subscribe, and was unable to compel them to do so, he sent for Hosius, and instead of banishing him, detained him a whole year in Sirmium. Godless, unholy, without natural affection, he feared not God, he regarded not his father's affection for Hosius, he reverenced not his great age, for he was now a hundred years old ; but all these things this modern Ahab, this second Belshazzar of our times, disregarded for the sake of impiety. He used such violence towards the old man, and confined him so tightly, that at last, broken by suffering, he was brought, though hardly, to hold communion with Valens, Ursacius, and their fellows, though he would not subscribe against Athanasius. Yet even thus he forgot not his duty, for at the approach of death, as it were by his last testament, he bore witness to the force which had been used towards him, and anathematized the Arian heresy, and gave strict charge that no one should receive it.

Arbitrary expulsion of so many bishops

Who that witnessed these things, or that has merely heard of them, will not be greatly amazed, and cry aloud unto the Lord, saying, 'Will You make a full end of Israel Ezekiel 11:13?' Who that is acquainted with these proceedings, will not with good reason cry out and say, 'A wonderful and horrible thing is done in the land;' and, 'The heavens are astonished at this, and the earth is even more horribly afraid. ' The fathers of the people and the teachers of the faith are taken away, and the impious are brought into the Churches? Who that saw when Liberius, Bishop of Rome, was banished, and when the great Hosius, the father of the Bishops, suffered these things, or who that saw so many Bishops banished out of Spain and the other parts, could fail to perceive, however little sense he might possess, that the charges against Athanasius also and the rest were false, and altogether mere calumny? For this reason those others also endured all suffering, because they saw plainly that the conspiracies laid against these were founded in falsehood. For what charge was there against Liberius? Or what accusation against the aged Hosius? Who bore even a false witness against Paulinus, and Lucifer, and Dionysius, and Eusebius? Or what sin could be lain to the account of the rest of the banished Bishops, and Presbyters, and Deacons? None whatever; God forbid. There were no charges against them on which a plot for their ruin might be formed; nor was it on the ground of any accusation that they were severally banished. It was an insurrection of impiety against godliness; it was zeal for the Arian heresy, and a prelude to the coming of Antichrist, for whom Constantius is thus preparing the way.

BOOK VII

Persecution at Alexandria

'After' he had accomplished all that he desired against the Churches in Italy, and the other parts; after he had banished some, and violently oppressed others, and filled every place with fear, he at last turned his fury, as it had been some pestilential disorder, against Alexandria. This was artfully contrived by the enemies of Christ; for in order that they might have a show of the signatures of many Bishops, and that Athanasius might not have a single Bishop in his persecution to whom he could even complain, they therefore anticipated his proceedings, and filled every place with terror, which they kept up to second them in the prosecution of their designs. But herein they perceived not through their folly that they were not exhibiting the deliberate choice of the Bishops, but rather the violence which themselves had employed; and that, although his brethren should desert him, and his friends and acquaintance stand afar off, and no one be found to sympathise with him and console him, yet far above all these, a refuge with his God was sufficient for him. For Elijah also was alone in his persecution, and God was all in all to the holy man. And the Saviour has given us an example herein, who also was left alone, and exposed to the designs of His enemies, to teach us, that when we are persecuted and deserted by men, we must not faint, but place our hope in Him, and not betray the Truth. For although at first truth may seem to be afflicted, yet even they who persecute shall afterwards acknowledge it.

Attacks upon the Alexandrian Church

Accordingly they urge on the Emperor, who first writes a menacing letter, which he sends to the Duke and the soldiers. The Notaries Diogenius and Hilarius , and certain Palatines with them, were the bearers of it; upon whose arrival those terrible and cruel outrages were committed against the Church, which I have briefly related a little above , and which are known to all men from the protests put forth by the people, which are inserted at the end of this history, so that any one may read them. Then after these proceedings on the part of Syrianus, after these enormities had been perpetrated, and violence offered to the Virgins, as approving of such conduct and the infliction of these evils upon us, he writes again to the senate and people of Alexandria, instigating the younger men, and requiring them to assemble together, and either to persecute Athanasius, or consider themselves as his enemies. He however had withdrawn before these instructions reached them, and from the time when Syrianus broke into the Church; for he remembered that which was written, 'Hide yourself as it were for a little moment, until the indignation be overpast Isaiah 26:20.' One Heraclius, by rank a Count, was the bearer of this letter, and the precursor of a certain George that was dispatched by the Emperor as a spy, for one that was sent from him cannot be a Bishop ; God forbid. And so indeed his conduct and the circumstances which preceded his entrance sufficiently prove.

Hypocrisy of the pretended respect of Constantius for his brother's memory

Heraclius then published the letter, which reflected great disgrace upon the writer. For whereas, when the great Hosius wrote to Constantius, he had been unable to make out any plausible pretext for his change of conduct, he now invented an excuse much more discreditable to himself and his advisers. He said, 'From regard to the affection I entertained towards my brother of divine and pious memory, I endured for a time the coming of Athanasius among you.' This proves that he has both broken his promise, and behaved ungratefully to his brother after his death. He then declares him to be, as indeed he is, 'deserving of divine and pious remembrance;' yet as regards a command of his, or to use his own language, the 'affection' he bore him, even though he complied merely 'for the sake' of the blessed Constans, he ought to deal fairly by his brother, and make himself heir to his sentiments as well as to the Empire. But, although, when seeking to obtain his just rights, he deposed Vetranio, with the question, 'To whom does the inheritance belong after a brother's death ?' yet for the sake of the accursed heresy of the enemies of Christ, he disregards the claims of justice, and behaves undutifully towards his brethren. Nay, for the sake of this heresy, he would not consent to observe even his father's wishes without infringement; but, in what he may gratify these impious men, he pretends to adopt his intention, while in order to distress the others, he cares not to show the reverence which is due unto a father. For in consequence of the calumnies of Eusebius and his fellows, his father sent the Bishop for a time into Gaul to avoid the cruelty of his persecutors (this was shown by the blessed Constantine, the brother of the former, after their father's death, as appears by his letters), but he would not be persuaded by Eusebius and his fellows to send the person whom they desired for a Bishop, but prevented the accomplishment of their wishes, and put a stop to their attempts with severe threats.

How Constantius shows his respect for his father and brother

If therefore, as he declares in his letters, he desired to observe his sire's practice, why did he first send out Gregory, and now this George, the eater of stores ? Why does he endeavour so earnestly to introduce into the Church these Arians, whom his father named Porphyrians , and banish others while he patronises them? Although his father admitted Arius to his presence, yet when Arius perjured himself and burst asunder he lost the compassion of his father; who, on learning the truth, condemned him as an heretic. Why moreover, while pretending to respect the Canon of the Church, has he ordered the whole course of his conduct in opposition to them? For where is there a Canon that a Bishop should be appointed from Court? Where is there a Canon that permits soldiers to invade Churches? What tradition is there allowing counts and ignorant eunuchs to exercise authority in Ecclesiastical matters, and to make known by their edicts the decisions of those who bear the name of Bishops? He is guilty of all manner of falsehood for the sake of this unholy heresy. At a former time he sent out Philagrius as Prefect a second time , in opposition to the opinion of his father, and we see what has taken place now. Nor 'for his brother's sake' does he speak the truth. For after his death he wrote not once nor twice, but three times to the Bishop, and repeatedly promised him that he would not change his behaviour towards him, but exhorted him to be of good courage, and not suffer any one to alarm him, but to continue to abide in his Church in perfect security. He also sent his commands by Count Asterius, and Palladius the Notary, to Felicissimus, who was then Duke, and to the Prefect Nestorius, that if either Philip the Prefect, or any other should venture to form any plot against Athanasius, they should prevent it.

The Emperor has no right to rule the Church

Wherefore when Diogenes came, and Syrianus laid in wait for us, both he and we and the people demanded to see the Emperor's letters, supposing that, as it is written, 'Let not a falsehood be spoken before the king ;' so when a king has made a promise, he will not lie, nor change. If then 'for his brother's sake he complied,' why did he also write those letters upon his death? And if he wrote them for 'his memory's sake,' why did he afterwards behave so very unkindly towards him, and persecute the man, and write what he did, alleging a judgment of Bishops, while in truth he acted only to please himself? Nevertheless his craft has not escaped detection, but we have the proof of it ready at hand. For if a judgment had been passed by Bishops, what concern had the Emperor with it? Or if it was only a threat of the Emperor, what need in that case was there of the so-named Bishops? When was such a thing heard of before from the beginning of the world? When did a judgment of the Church receive its validity from the Emperor? Or rather when was his decree ever recognised by the Church? There have been many Councils held heretofore; and many judgments passed by the Church; but the Fathers never sought the consent of the Emperor thereto, nor did the Emperor busy himself with the affairs of the

Church. The Apostle Paul had friends among them of Cæsar's household, and in his Epistle to the Philippians he sent salutations from them; but he never took them as his associates in Ecclesiastical judgments. Now however we have witnessed a novel spectacle, which is a discovery of the Arian heresy. Heretics have assembled together with the Emperor Constantius, in order that he, alleging the authority of the Bishops, may exercise his power against whomsoever he pleases, and while he persecutes may avoid the name of persecutor; and that they, supported by the Emperor's government, may conspire the ruin of whomsoever they will and these are all such as are not as impious as themselves. One might look upon their proceedings as a comedy which they are performing on the stage, in which the pretended Bishops are actors, and Constantius the performer of their behests, who makes promises to them, as Herod did to the daughter of Herodias, and they dancing before him accomplish through false accusations the banishment and death of the true believers in the Lord.

Despotic interference of Constantius

Who indeed has not been injured by their calumnies? Whom have not these enemies of Christ conspired to destroy? Whom has Constantius failed to banish upon charges which they have brought against them? When did he refuse to hear them willingly? And what is most strange, when did he permit any one to speak against them, and did not more readily receive their testimony, of whatever kind it might be? Where is there a Church which now enjoys the privilege of worshipping Christ freely? If a Church be a maintainer of true piety, it is in danger; if it dissemble, it abides in fear. Every place is full of hypocrisy and impiety, so far as he is concerned; and wherever there is a pious person and a lover of Christ (and there are many such everywhere, as were the prophets and the great Elijah) they hide themselves, if so be that they can find a faithful friend like Obadiah, and either they withdraw into caves and dens of the earth, or pass their lives in wandering about in the deserts. These men in their madness prefer such calumnies against them as Jezebel invented against Naboth, and the Jews against the Saviour; while the Emperor, who is the patron of the heresy, and wishes to pervert the truth, as Ahab wished to change the vineyard into a garden of herbs, does whatever they desire him to do, for the suggestions he receives from them are agreeable to his own wishes.

Constantius gives up the Alexandrian Churches to the heretics

Accordingly he banished, as I said before the genuine Bishops, because they would not profess impious doctrines, to suit his own pleasure; and so he now sent Count Heraclius to proceed against Athanasius, who has publicly made known his decrees, and announced the command of the Emperor to be, that unless they complied with the instructions contained in his letters, their bread should be taken away, their idols overthrown, and the persons of many of the city-magistrates and people delivered over to certain slavery. After threatening them in this manner, he was not ashamed to declare publicly with a loud voice, 'The Emperor disclaims Athanasius, and has commanded that the Churches be given up to the Arians.' And when all wondered to hear this, and made signs to one another, exclaiming, 'What! Has Constantius become a heretic?' instead of blushing as he ought, the man all the more obliged the senators and heathen magistrates and wardens of the idol temples to subscribe to these conditions, and to agree to receive as their Bishop whomsoever the Emperor should send them. Of course Constantius was strictly upholding the Canon of the Church, when he caused this to be done; when instead of requiring letters from the Church, he demanded them of the market-place, and instead of the people he asked them of the wardens of the temples. He was conscious that he was not sending a Bishop to preside over Christians, but a certain intruder for those who subscribed to his terms.

History of the arians ~ Athanasius of Alexandria

Irruption into the great Church

The Gentiles accordingly, as purchasing by their compliance the safety of their idols, and certain of the trades , subscribed, though unwillingly, from fear of the threats which he had held out to them; just as if the matter had been the appointment of a general, or other magistrate. Indeed what as heathen, were they likely to do, except whatever was pleasing to the Emperor? But the people having assembled in the great Church (for it was the fourth day of the week), Count Heraclius on the following day takes with him Cataphronius the Prefect of Egypt, and Faustinus the Receiver-General , and Bithynus a heretic; and together they stir up the younger men of the common multitude who worshipped idols, to attack the Church, and stone the people, saying that such was the Emperor's command. As the time of dismissal however had arrived, the greater part had already left the Church, but there being a few women still remaining, they did as the men had charged them, whereupon a piteous spectacle ensued. The few women had just risen from prayer and had sat down when the youths suddenly came upon them naked with stones and clubs. Some of them the godless wretches stoned to death; they scourged with stripes the holy persons of the Virgins, tore off their veils and exposed their heads, and when they resisted the insult, the cowards kicked them with their feet. This was dreadful, exceedingly dreadful; but what ensued was worse, and more intolerable than any outrage. Knowing the holy character of the virgins, and that their ears were unaccustomed to pollution, and that they were better able to bear stones and swords than expressions of obscenity, they assailed them with such language. This the Arians suggested to the young men, and laughed at all they said and did; while the holy Virgins and other godly women fled from such words as they would from the bite of asps, but the enemies of Christ assisted them in the work, nay even, it may be, gave utterance to the same; for they were well-pleased with the obscenities which the youths vented upon them.

The great Church pillaged

After this, that they might fully execute the orders they had received (for this was what they earnestly desired, and what the Count and the Receiver-General instructed them to do), they seized upon the seats, the throne, and the table which was of wood , and the curtains of the Church, and whatever else they were able, and carrying them out burnt them before the doors in the great street, and cast frankincense upon the flame. Alas! Who will not weep to hear of these things, and, it may be, close his ears, that he may not have to endure the recital, esteeming it hurtful merely to listen to the account of such enormities? Moreover they sang the praises of their idols, and said, 'Constantius has become a heathen, and the Arians have acknowledged our customs;' for indeed they scruple not even to pretend heathenism, if only their heresy may be established. They even were ready to sacrifice a heifer which drew the water for the gardens in the Cæsareum ; and would have sacrificed it, had it not been a female ; for they said that it was unlawful for such to be offered among them.

57. Thus acted the impious Arians in conjunction with the heathens, thinking that these things tended to our dishonour. But Divine justice reproved their iniquity, and wrought a great and remarkable sign, thereby plainly showing to all men, that as in their acts of

impiety they had dared to attack none other but the Lord, so in these proceedings also they were again attempting to do dishonour unto Him. This was more manifestly proved by the marvellous event which now came to pass. One of these licentious youths ran into the Church, and ventured to sit down upon the throne; and as he sat there the wretched man uttered with a nasal sound some lascivious song. Then rising up he attempted to pull away the throne, and to drag it towards him; he knew not that he was drawing down vengeance upon himself. For as of old the inhabitants of Azotus, when they ventured to touch the Ark, which it was not lawful for them even to look upon, were immediately destroyed by it, being first grievously tormented by emerods; so this unhappy person who presumed to drag the throne, drew it upon himself, and, as if Divine justice had sent the wood to punish him, he struck it into his own bowels; and instead of carrying out the throne, he brought out by his blow his own entrails; so that the throne took away his life, instead of his taking it away. For, as it is Acts 1:18 written of Judas, his bowels gushed out; and he fell down and was carried away, and the day after he died. Another also entered the Church with boughs of trees and, as in the Gentile manner he waved them in his hands and mocked, he was immediately struck with blindness, so as straightway to lose his sight, and to know no longer where he was; but as he was about to fall, he was taken by the hand and supported by his companions out of the place, and when on the following day he was with difficulty brought to his senses, he knew not either what he had done or suffered in consequence of his audacity.

General Persecution at Alexandria

The Gentiles, when they beheld these things, were seized with fear, and ventured on no further outrage; but the Arians were not even yet touched with shame, but, like the Jews when they saw the miracles, were faithless and would not believe, nay, like Pharaoh, they were hardened; they too having placed their hopes below, on the Emperor and his eunuchs. They permitted the Gentiles, or rather the more abandoned of the Gentiles, to act in the manner before described; for they found that Faustinus, who is the Receiver-General by style, but is a vulgar person in habits, and profligate in heart, was ready to play his part with them in these proceedings, and to stir up the heathen. Nay, they undertook to do the like themselves, that as they had modelled their heresy upon all other heresies together , so they might share their wickedness with the more depraved of mankind. What they did through the instrumentality of others I described above; the enormities they committed themselves surpass the bounds of all wickedness; and they exceed the malice of any hangman. Where is there a house which they did not ravage? Where is there a family they did not plunder on pretence of searching for their opponents? Where is there a garden they did not trample under foot? What tomb did they not open, pretending they were seeking for Athanasius, though their sole object was to plunder and spoil all that came in their way? How many men's houses were sealed up! The contents of how many persons' lodgings did they give away to the soldiers who assisted them! Who had not experience of their wickedness? Who that met them but was obliged to hide himself in the market-place? Did not many an one leave his house from fear of them, and pass the night in the desert? Did not many an one, while anxious to preserve his property from them, lose the greater part of it? And who, however inexperienced of the sea, did not choose rather to commit himself to it, and to risk all its dangers, than to witness their threatenings? Many also changed their residences, and removed from street to street, and from the city to the suburbs. And many submitted to severe fines, and when they were unable to pay, borrowed of others, merely that they might escape their machinations.

Violence of Sebastianus

For they made themselves formidable to all men, and treated all with great arrogance, using the name of the Emperor, and threatening them with his displeasure. They had to assist them in their wickedness the Duke Sebastianus, a Manichee, and a profligate young man; the Prefect, the Count, and the Receiver-General as a dissembler. Many Virgins who condemned their impiety, and professed the truth, they brought out from the houses; others they insulted as they walked along the streets, and caused their heads to be uncovered by their young men. They also gave permission to the females of their party to insult whom they chose; and although the holy and faithful women withdrew on one side, and gave them the way, yet they gathered round them like Bacchanals and Furies , and esteemed it a misfortune if they found no means to injure them, and spent that day sorrowfully on which they were unable to do them some mischief. In a word, so cruel and bitter were they against all, that all men called them hangmen, murderers, lawless, intruders, evil-doers, and by any other name rather than that of Christians.

History of the arians ~ Athanasius of Alexandria

Martyrdom of Eutychius

Moreover, imitating the savage practices of Scythians, they seized upon Eutychius a Subdeacon, a man who had served the Church honourably, and causing him to be scourged on the back with a leather whip, till he was at the point of death, they demanded that her should be sent away to the mines; and not simply to any mine, but to that of Phæno , where even a condemned murderer is hardly able to live a few days. And what was most unreasonable in their conduct, they would not permit him even a few hours to have his wounds dressed, but caused him to be sent off immediately, saying, 'If this is done, all men will be afraid, and henceforward will be on our side.' After a short interval, however, being unable to accomplish his journey to the mine on account of the pain of his stripes, he died on the way. He perished rejoicing, having obtained the glory of martyrdom. But the miscreants were not even yet ashamed, but in the words of Scripture, 'having bowels without mercy Proverbs 12:10,' they acted accordingly, and now again perpetrated a satanic deed. When the people prayed them to spare Eutychius and besought them for him, they caused four honourable and free citizens to be seized, one of whom was Hermias who washed the beggars' feet ; and after scourging them very severely, the Duke cast them into the prison. But the Arians, who are more cruel even than Scythians, when they had seen that they did not die from the stripes they had received, complained of the Duke and threatened, saying, 'We will write and tell the eunuchs , that he does not flog as we wish.' Hearing this he was afraid, and was obliged to beat the men a second time; and they being beaten, and knowing for what cause they suffered and by whom they had been accused, said only, 'We are beaten for the sake of the Truth, but we will not hold communion with the heretics: beat us now as you will; God will judge you for this.' The impious men wished to expose them to danger in the prison, that they might die there; but the people of God observing their time, besought him for them, and after seven days or more they were set at liberty.

Ill-treatment of the poor

But the Arians, as being grieved at this, again devised another yet more cruel and unholy deed; cruel in the eyes of all men, but well suited to their antichristian heresy. The Lord commanded that we should remember the poor; He said, 'Sell that you have, and give alms' and again 'I was a hungred, and you gave Me meat; I was thirsty, and you gave Me drink; for inasmuch as you have done it unto one of these little ones, you have done it unto Me. ' But these men, as being in truth opposed to Christ, have presumed to act contrary to His will in this respect also. For when the Duke gave up the Churches to the Arians, and the destitute persons and widows were unable to continue any longer in them, the widows sat down in places which the Clergy entrusted with the care of them appointed. And when the Arians saw that the brethren readily ministered unto them and supported them, they persecuted the widows also, beating them on the feet, and accused those who gave to them before the Duke. This was done by means of a certain soldier named Dynamius. And it was well-pleasing to Sebastian , for there is no mercy in the Manichæans; nay, it is considered a hateful thing among them to show mercy to a poor man. Here then was a novel subject of complaint; and a new kind of court now first invented by the Arians. Persons were brought to trial for acts of kindness which they had performed;

he who showed mercy was accused, and he who had received a benefit was beaten; and they wished rather that a poor man should suffer hunger, than that he who was willing to show mercy should give to him. Such sentiments these modern Jews, for such they are, have learned from the Jews of old, who when they saw him who had been blind from his birth recover his sight, and him who had been a long time sick of the palsy made whole, accused the Lord who had bestowed these benefits upon them, and judged them to be transgressors who had experienced His goodness.

Ill-treatment of the poor

Who was not struck with astonishment at these proceedings? Who did not execrate both the heresy, and its defenders? Who failed to perceive that the Arians are indeed more cruel than wild beasts? For they had no prospect of gain from their iniquity, for the sake of which they might have acted in this manner; but they rather increased the hatred of all men against themselves. They thought by treachery and terror to force certain persons into their heresy, so that they might be brought to communicate with them; but the event turned out quite the contrary. The sufferers endured as martyrdom whatever they inflicted upon them, and neither betrayed nor denied the true faith in Christ. And those who were without and witnessed their conduct, and at last even the heathen, when they saw these things, execrated them as antichristian, as cruel executioners; for human nature is prone to pity and sympathise with the poor. But these men have lost even the common sentiments of humanity; and that kindness which they would have desired to meet with at the hands of others, had themselves been sufferers, they would not permit others to receive, but employed against them the severity and authority of the magistrates, and especially of the Duke.

Ill-treatment of the Presbyters and Deacons

What they have done to the Presbyters and Deacons; how they drove them into banishment under sentence passed upon them by the Duke and the magistrates, causing the soldiers to bring out their kinsfolk from the houses , and Gorgonius, the commander of the police to beat them with stripes; and how (most cruel act of all) with much insolence they plundered the loaves of these and of those who were now dead; these things it is impossible for words to describe, for their cruelty surpasses all the powers of language. What terms could one employ which might seem equal to the subject? What circumstances could one mention first, so that those next recorded would not be found more dreadful, and the next more dreadful still? All their attempts and iniquities were full of murder and impiety; and so unscrupulous and artful are they, that they endeavour to deceive by promises of protection, and by bribing with money , that so, since they cannot recommend themselves by fair means, they may thereby make some display to impose on the simple.

History of the arians ~ Athanasius of Alexandria

BOOK VIII

Persecution in Egypt

64. Who would call them even by the name of Gentiles; much less by that of Christians? Would any one regard their habits and feelings as human, and not rather those of wild beasts, seeing their cruel and savage conduct? They are more worthless than public hangmen; more audacious than all other heretics. To the Gentiles they are much inferior, and stand far apart and separate from them. I have heard from our fathers, and I believe their report to be a faithful one, that long ago, when a persecution arose in the time of Maximian, the grandfather of Constantius, the Gentiles concealed our brethren the Christians, who were sought after, and frequently suffered the loss of their own substance, and had trial of imprisonment, solely that they might not betray the fugitives. They protected those who fled to them for refuge, as they would have done their own persons, and were determined to run all risks on their behalf. But now these admirable persons, the inventors of a new heresy, act altogether the contrary part; and are distinguished for nothing but their treachery. They have appointed themselves as executioners, and seek to betray all alike, and make those who conceal others

the objects of their plots, esteeming equally as their enemy both him that conceals and him that is concealed. So murderous are they; so emulous in their evil-doings of the wickedness of Judas.

History of the arians ~ Athanasius of Alexandria

Martyrdom of Secundus of Barka

The crimes these men have committed cannot adequately be described. I would only say, that as I write and wish to enumerate all their deeds of iniquity, the thought enters my mind, whether this heresy be not the fourth daughter of the horse-leach Proverbs 30:15 in the Proverbs, since after so many acts of injustice, so many murders, it has not yet said, 'It is enough.' No; it still rages, and goes about seeking after those whom it has not yet discovered, while those whom it has already injured, it is eager to injure anew. After the night attack, after the evils committed in consequence of it, after the persecution brought about by Heraclius, they cease not yet to accuse us falsely before the Emperor (and they are confident that as impious persons they will obtain a hearing), desiring that something more than banishment may be inflicted upon us, and that hereafter those who do not consent to their impieties may be destroyed. Accordingly, being now emboldened in an extreme degree, that most abandoned Secundus of Pentapolis, and Stephanus his accomplice, conscious that their heresy was a defence of any injustice they might commit, on discovering a Presbyter at Barka who would not comply with their desires (he was called Secundus, being of the same name, but not of the same faith with the heretic), they kicked him till he died. While he was thus suffering he imitated the Saint, and said, 'Let no one avenge my cause before human judges; I have the Lord for my avenger, for whose sake I suffer these things at their hands.' They however were not moved with pity at these words, nor did they feel any awe of the sacred season; for it was during the time of Lent that they thus kicked the man to death.

History of the arians ~ Athanasius of Alexandria

Persecution the weapon of Arianism

O new heresy, that hast put on the whole devil in impiety and wicked deeds! For in truth it is but a lately invented evil; and although certain heretofore appear to have adopted its doctrines, yet they concealed them, and were not known to hold them. But Eusebius and Arius, like serpents coming out of their holes, have vomited forth the poison of this impiety; Arius daring to blaspheme openly, and Eusebius defending his blasphemy. He was not however able to support the heresy, until, as I said before, he found a patron for it in the Emperor. Our fathers called an Ecumenical Council, when three hundred of them, more or less , met together and condemned the Arian heresy, and all declared that it was alien and strange to the faith of the Church. Upon this its supporters, perceiving that they were dishonoured, and had now no good ground of argument to insist upon, devised a different method, and attempted to vindicate it by means of external power. And herein one may especially admire the novelty as well as wickedness of their device, and how they go beyond all other heresies. For these support their madness by persuasive arguments calculated to deceive the simple; the Greeks, as the Apostle has said, make their attack with excellency and persuasiveness of speech, and with plausible fallacies; the Jews, leaving the divine Scriptures, now, as the Apostle again has said, contend about 'fables and endless genealogies 1 Timothy 1:4;' and the Manichees and Valentinians with them, and others, corrupting the divine Scriptures, put forth fables in terms of their own inventions. But the Arians are bolder than them all, and have shown that the other heresies are but their younger sisters , whom, as I have said, they surpass in impiety, emulating them all, and especially the Jews in their iniquity. For as the Jews, when they were unable to prove the charges which they pretended to allege against Paul, straightway led him to the chief captain and the governor; so likewise these men, who surpass the Jews in their devices, make use only of the power of the judges; and if any one so much as speaks against them, he is dragged before the Governor or the General.

Arianism worse than other heresies, because of Persecution

The other heresies also, when the very Truth has refuted them on the clearest evidence, are wont to be silent, being simply confounded by their conviction. But this modern and accursed heresy, when it is overthrown by argument, when it is cast down and covered with shame by the very Truth, immediately endeavours to coerce by violence and stripes and imprisonment those whom it has been unable to persuade by argument, thereby acknowledging itself to be anything rather than godly. For it is the part of true godliness not to compel , but to persuade, as I said before. Thus our Lord Himself, not as employing force, but as offering to their free choice, has said to all, 'If any man will follow after Me Matthew 16:24;' and to His disciples, 'Will you also go away John 6:67?' This heresy, however, is altogether alien from godliness; and therefore how otherwise should it act, than contrary to our Saviour, seeing also that it has enlisted that enemy of Christ, Constantius, as it were Antichrist himself , to be its leader in impiety? He for its sake has earnestly endeavoured to emulate Saul in savage cruelty. For when the priests gave victuals to David, Saul commanded, and they were all destroyed, in number three hundred and five ; and this man, now that all avoid the heresy, and confess a sound faith in the Lord, annuls a Council of full three hundred Bishops, banishes the Bishops themselves, and hinders the people from the practice of piety, and from their prayers to God, preventing their public assemblies. And as Saul overthrew Nob, the city of the priests, so this man, advancing even further in wickedness, has given up the Churches to the impious. And as he honoured Doeg the accuser before the true priests, and persecuted David, giving ear to the Ziphites; so this man prefers heretics to the godly, and still persecutes them that flee from him, giving ear to his own eunuchs, who falsely accuse the orthodox. He does not perceive that whatever he does or writes in behalf of the heresy of the Arians, involves an attack upon the Saviour.

Constantius worse than Saul, Ahab, and Pilate. His past conduct to his own relations

Ahab himself did not act so cruelly towards the priests of God, as this man has acted towards the Bishops. For he was at least pricked in his conscience, when Naboth had been murdered, and was afraid at the sight 1 Kings 21:20 of Elijah, but this man neither reverenced the great Hosius, nor was wearied or pricked in conscience, after banishing so many Bishops; but like another Pharaoh, the more he is afflicted, the more he is hardened, and imagines greater wickedness day by day. And the most extraordinary instance of his iniquity was the following. It happened that when the Bishops were condemned to banishment, certain other persons also received their sentence on charges of murder or sedition or theft, each according to the quality of his offense. These men after a few months he released, on being requested to do so, as Pilate did Barabbas; but the servants of Christ he not only refused to set at liberty, but even sentenced them to more unmerciful punishment in the place of their exile, proving himself 'an undying evil ' to them. To the others through congeniality of disposition he became a friend; but to the orthodox he was an enemy on account of their true faith in Christ. Is it not clear to all men from hence, that the Jews of old when they demanded Barabbas, and crucified the Lord, acted but the part which these present enemies of Christ are acting together with Constantius? Nay, that he is even more bitter than Pilate. For Pilate, when he perceived Matthew 27:24 the injustice of the deed, washed his hands; but this man, while he banishes the saints, gnashes his teeth against them more and more.

69. But what wonder is it if, after he has been led into impious errors, he is so cruel towards the Bishops, since the common feelings of humanity could not induce him to spare even his own kindred. His uncles he slew; his cousins he put out of the way; he commiserated not the sufferings of his father-in-law, though he had married his daughter, or of his kinsmen; but he has ever been a transgressor of his oaths towards all. So likewise he treated his brother in an unholy manner; and now he pretends to build his sepulchre, although he delivered up to the barbarians his betrothed wife Olympias, whom his brother had protected till his death, and had brought up as his intended consort. Moreover he attempted to set aside his wishes, although he boasts to be his heir ; for so he writes, in terms which any one possessed of but a small measure of sense would be ashamed of. But when I compare his letters, I find that he does not possess common understanding, but that his mind is solely regulated by the suggestions of others, and that he has no mind of his own at all. Now Solomon says, 'If a ruler hearken to lies, all his servants are wicked

Proverbs 29:12.' This man proves by his actions that he is such an unjust one, and that those about him are wicked.

Inconstancy of Constantius

How then, being such an one, and taking pleasure in such associates, can he ever design anything just or reasonable, entangled as he is in the iniquity of his followers, men who verily bewitch him, or rather who have trampled his brains under their heels? Wherefore he now writes letters , and then repents that he has written them, and after repenting is again stirred up to anger, and then again laments his fate, and being undetermined what to do, he shows a soul destitute of understanding. Being then of such a character, one must fairly pity him, because that under the semblance and name of freedom he is the slave of those who drag him on to gratify their own impious pleasure. In a word, while through his folly and inconstancy, as the Scripture says , he is willing to comply with the desires of others, he has given himself up to condemnation, to be consumed by fire in the future judgment; at once consenting to do whatever they wish, and gratifying them in their designs against the Bishops, and in their exertion of authority over the Churches. For behold, he has now again thrown into disorder all the Churches of Alexandria and of Egypt and Libya, and has publicly given orders, that the Bishops of the Catholic Church and faith be cast out of their churches, and that they be all given up to the professors of the Arian doctrines. The General began to carry this order into execution; and straightway Bishops were sent off in chains, and Presbyters and Monks bound with iron, after being almost beaten to death with stripes. Disorder prevails in every place; all Egypt and Libya are in danger, the people being indignant at this unjust command, and seeing in it the preparation for the coming of Antichrist, and beholding their property plundered by others, and given up into the hands of the heretics.

This wickedness unprecedented

When was ever such iniquity heard of? When was such an evil deed ever perpetrated, even in times of persecution? They were heathens who persecuted formerly; but they did not bring their idols into the Churches. Zenobia , was a Jewess, and a supporter of Paul of Samosata; but she did not give up the Churches to the Jews for Synagogues. This is a new piece of iniquity. It is not simply persecution, but more than persecution, it is a prelude and preparation for the coming of Antichrist. Even if it be admitted that they invented false charges against Athanasius and the rest of the Bishops whom they banished, yet what is this to their later practices? What charges have they to allege against the whole of Egypt and Libya and Pentapolis ? For they have begun no longer to lay their plots against individuals, in which case they might be able to frame a lie against them; but they have set upon all in a body, so that if they merely choose to invent accusations against them, they must be condemned. Thus their wickedness has blinded their understanding Wisdom 2:21; and they have required, without any reason assigned, that the whole body of the Bishops shall be expelled, and thereby they show that the charges they framed against Athanasius and the rest of the Bishops whom they banished were false, and invented for no other purpose than to support the accursed heresy of the

Arian enemies of Christ. This is now no longer concealed, but has become most manifest to all men. He commanded Athanasius to be expelled out of the city, and gave up the Churches to them. And the Presbyters and Deacons that were with him, who had been appointed by Peter and Alexander, were also expelled and driven into banishment; and the real Arians, who not through any suspicions arising from circumstances, but on account of the heresy had been expelled at first together with Arius himself by the Bishop Alexander,— Secundus in Libya, in Alexandria Euzoius the Chananæan, Julius, Ammon, Marcus, Irenæus, Zosimus, and Sarapion surnamed Pelycon, and in Libya Sisinnius, and the younger men with him, associates in his impiety; these have obtained possession of the Churches.

Banishment of Egyptian Bishops

And the General Sebastian wrote to the governors and military authorities in every place; and the true Bishops were persecuted, and those who professed impious doctrines were brought in in their stead. They banished Bishops who had grown old in orders, and had been many years in the Episcopate, having been ordained by the Bishop Alexander; Ammonius, Hermes, Anagamphus, and Marcus, they sent to the Upper Oasis; Muis, Psenosiris, Nilammon, Plenes, Marcus, and Athenodorus to Ammoniaca, with no other intention than that they should perish in their passage through the deserts. They had no pity on them though they were suffering from illness, and indeed proceeded on their journey with so much difficulty on account of their weakness, that they were obliged to be carried in litters, and their sickness was so dangerous that the materials for their burial accompanied them. One of them indeed died, but they would not even permit the body to be given up to his friends for interment. With the same purpose they banished also the Bishop Dracontius to the desert places about Clysma, Philo to Babylon, Adelphius to Psinabla in the Thebais, and the Presbyters Hierax and Dioscorus to Syene. They likewise drove into exile Ammonius, Agathus, Agathodæmon, Apollonius, Eulogius, Apollos, Paphnutius, Gaius, and Flavius, ancient Bishops, as also the Bishops

History of the arians ~ Athanasius of Alexandria

Dioscorus, Ammonius, Heraclides, and Psais; some of whom they gave up to work in the stone-quarries, others they persecuted with an intention to destroy, and many others they plundered. They banished also forty of the laity, with certain virgins whom they had before exposed to the fire ; beating them so severely with rods taken from palm-trees, that after lingering five days some of them died, and others had recourse to surgical treatment on account of the thorns left in their limbs, from which they suffered torments worse than death. But what is most dreadful to the mind of any man of sound understanding, though characteristic of these miscreants, is this: When the virgins during the scourging called upon the Name of Christ, they gnashed their teeth against them with increased fury. Nay more, they would not give up the bodies of the dead to their friends for burial, but concealed them that they might appear to be ignorant of the murder. They did not however escape detection; the whole city perceived it, and all men withdrew from them as executioners, as malefactors and robbers. Moreover they overthrew monasteries, and endeavoured to cast monks into the fire; they plundered houses, and breaking into the house of certain free citizens where the Bishop had deposited a treasure, they plundered and took it away. They scourged the widows on the soles of their feet, and hindered them from receiving their alms.

Character of Ariannominees

Such were the iniquities practised by the Arians; and as to their further deeds of impiety, who could hear the account of them without shuddering? They had caused these venerable old men and aged Bishops to be sent into banishment; they now appointed in their stead profligate heathen youths, whom they thought to raise at once to the highest dignity, though they were not even Catechumens. And others who were accused of bigamy , and even of worse crimes, they nominated Bishops on account of the wealth and civil power which they possessed, and sent them out as it were from a market, upon their giving them gold. And now more dreadful calamities befell the people. For when they rejected these mercenary dependents of the Arians, so alien from themselves, they were scourged, they were proscribed, they were shut up in prison by the General (who did all this readily, being a Manichee), in order that they might no longer seek after their own Bishops, but be forced to accept those whom they abominated, men who were now guilty of the same mockeries as they had before practised among their idols.

History of the arians ~ Athanasius of Alexandria

The Episcopal appointments of Constantius a mark of Antichrist

Will not every just person break forth into lamentations at the sight or hearing of these things, at perceiving the arrogance and extreme injustice of these impious men? 'The righteous lament in the place of the impious. ' After all these things, and now that the impiety has reached such a pitch of audacity, who will any longer venture to call this Costyllius a Christian, and not rather the image of Antichrist? For what mark of Antichrist is yet wanting? How can he in any way fail to be regarded as that one? Or how can the latter fail to be supposed such a one as he is? Did not the Arians and the Gentiles offer those sacrifices in the great Church in the Cæsareum , and utter their blasphemies against Christ as by His command? And does not the vision of Daniel thus describe Daniel 7:25 Antichrist; that he shall make war with the saints, and prevail against them, and exceed all that have been before him in evil deeds and shall humble three kings, and speak words against the Most High, and shall think to change times and laws? Now what other person besides Constantius has ever attempted to do these things? He is surely such a one as Antichrist would be. He speaks words against the Most High by supporting this impious heresy: he makes war against the saints by banishing the

143

Bishops; although indeed he exercises this power but for a little while to his own destruction. Moreover he has surpassed those before him in wickedness, having devised a new mode of persecution; and after he had overthrown three kings, namely Vetranio, Magnentius, and Gallus, he straightway undertook the patronage of impiety; and like a giant he has dared in his pride to set himself up against the Most High. He has thought to change laws, by transgressing the ordinance of the Lord given us through His Apostles, by altering the customs of the Church, and inventing a new kind of appointments. For he sends from strange places, distant a fifty days' journey , Bishops attended by soldiers to people unwilling to receive them; and instead of an introduction to the acquaintance of their people, they bring with them threatening messages and letters to the magistrates. Thus he sent Gregory from Cappadocia to Alexandria; he transferred Germinius from Cyzicus to Sirmium; he removed Cecropius from Laodicea to Nicomedia.

Arrival of George at Alexandria, and proceedings of Constantius in Italy

Again he transferred from Cappadocia to Milan one Auxentius , an intruder rather than a Christian, whom he commanded to stay there, after he had banished for his piety towards Christ Dionysius the Bishop of the place, a godly man. But this person was as yet even ignorant of the Latin language, and unskilful in everything except impiety. And now one George, a Cappadocian, who was contractor of stores at Constantinople, and having embezzled all monies that he received, was obliged to fly, he commanded to enter Alexandria with military pomp, and supported by the authority of the General. Next, finding one Epictetus a novice, a bold young man, he loved him , perceiving that he was ready for wickedness; and by his means he carries on his designs against those of the Bishops whom he desires to ruin. For he is prepared to do everything that the Emperor wishes; who accordingly availing himself of his assistance, has committed at Rome a strange act, but one truly resembling the malice of Antichrist. Having made preparations in the Palace instead of the Church, and caused some three of his own eunuchs to attend instead of the people, he then compelled three ill-conditioned spies (for one cannot call them Bishops), to ordain forsooth as Bishop one Felix , a man worthy of them, then in the Palace. For the people perceiving the iniquitous proceedings of the heretics would not allow them to enter the Churches , and withdrew themselves far from them.

Tyrannous banishment of Bishops by Constantius

Now what is yet wanting to make him Antichrist? Or what more could Antichrist do at his coming than this man has done? Will he not find when he comes that the way has been already prepared for him by this man easily to deceive the people? Again, he claims to himself the right of deciding causes, which he refers to the Court instead of the Church, and presides at them in person. And strange it is to say, when he perceives the accusers at a loss, he takes up the accusation himself, so that the injured party may no longer be able to defend himself on account of the violence which he displays. This he did in the proceedings against Athanasius. For when he saw the boldness of the Bishops Paulinus, Lucifer, Eusebius, and Dionysius, and how out of the recantation of Ursacius and Valens they confuted those who spoke against the Bishop, and advised that Valens and his fellows should no longer be believed, since they had already retracted what they now asserted, he immediately stood up and said, 'I am now the accuser of Athanasius; on my account you must believe what these assert.' And then, when they said—'But how can you be an accuser, when the accused person is not present? For if you are his accuser, yet he is not present, and therefore cannot be tried. And the cause is not one that concerns Rome, so that you should be believed as being the Emperor; but it is a matter that concerns a Bishop; for the trial ought to be conducted on equal terms both to the accuser and the accused. And besides, how can you accuse him? For you could not be present to witness the conduct of one who lived at so great a distance from you; and if you speak but what you have heard from these, you ought also to give credit to what he says; but if you will not believe him, while you do believe them, it is plain that they assert these things for your sake, and accuse Athanasius only to gratify you?'— when he heard this, thinking that what they had so truly spoken was an insult to himself, he sent them into banishment; and being exasperated against Athanasius, he wrote in a more savage strain, requiring that he should suffer what has now befallen him, and that the Churches should be given up to the Arians, and that they should be allowed to do whatever they pleased.

Constantius the precursor of Antichrist

Terrible indeed, and worse than terrible are such proceedings; yet conduct suitable to him who assumes the character of Antichrist. Who that beheld him taking the lead of his pretended Bishops, and presiding in Ecclesiastical causes, would not justly exclaim that this was 'the abomination of desolation Daniel 9:27 ' spoken of by Daniel? For having put on the profession of Christianity, and entering into the holy places, and standing therein, he lays waste the Churches, transgressing their Canons, and enforcing the observance of his own decrees. Will any one now venture to say that this is a peaceful time with Christians, and not a time of persecution? A persecution indeed, such as never arose before, and such as no one perhaps will again stir up, except 'the son of lawlessness 2 Thessalonians 2:8,' do these enemies of Christ exhibit, who already present a picture of him in their own persons. Wherefore it especially behooves us to be sober, lest this heresy which has reached such a height of impudence, and has diffused itself abroad like the 'poison of an adder Proverbs 23:32,' as it is written in the Proverbs, and which teaches doctrines contrary to the Saviour; lest, I say, this be that 'falling away 2 Thessalonians 2:3,' after which He shall be revealed, of whom

Constantius is surely the forerunner. Else why is he so mad against the godly? Why does he contend for it as his own heresy, and call every one his enemy who will not comply with the madness of Arius, and admit gladly the allegations of the enemies of Christ, and dishonour so many venerable Councils? Why did he command that the Churches should be given up to the Arians? Was it not that, when that other comes, he may thus find a way to enter into them, and may take to himself him who has prepared those places for him? For the ancient Bishops who were ordained by Alexander, and by his predecessor Achillas, and by Peter before him, have been cast out; and those introduced whom the companions of soldiers nominated; and they nominated only such as promised to adopt their doctrines.

Alliance of Meletians with Arians

This was an easy proposition for the Meletians to comply with; for the greater part, or rather the whole of them, have never had a religious education, nor are they acquainted with the 'sound faith ' in Christ, nor do they know at all what Christianity is, or what writings we Christians possess. For having come out, some of them from the worship of idols, and others from the senate, or from the first civil offices, for the sake of the miserable exemption from duty and for the patronage they gained, and having bribed the Meletians who preceded them, they have been advanced to this dignity even before they had been under instruction. And even if they pretended to have been such, yet what kind of instruction is to be obtained among the Meletians? But indeed without even pretending to be under instruction, they came at once, and immediately were called Bishops, just as children receive a name. Being then persons of this description, they thought the thing of no great consequence, nor even supposed that piety was different from impiety. Accordingly from being Meletians they readily and speedily became Arians; and if the Emperor should command them to adopt any other profession, they are ready to change again to that also. Their ignorance of true godliness quickly brings them to submit to the prevailing folly, and that which happens to be first taught them. For it is nothing to them to be carried about by every wind and tempest, so long as they are only exempt from duty, and obtain the patronage of men; nor would they scruple probably to change again to what they were before, even to become such as they were when they were heathens. Any how, being men of such an easy temper, and considering the Church as a civil senate, and like heathen being idolatrously minded, they put on the honourable name of the Saviour, under which they polluted the whole of Egypt, by causing so much as the name of the Arian heresy to be known therein. For Egypt has heretofore been the only country, throughout which the profession of the orthodox faith was boldly maintained ; and therefore these misbelievers have striven to introduce jealousy there also, or rather not they, but the devil who has stirred them up, in order that when his herald Antichrist shall come, he may find that the Churches in Egypt also are his own, and that the Meletians have already been instructed in his principles, and may recognise himself as already formed in them.

History of the arians ~ Athanasius of Alexandria

Behaviour of the Meletians contrasted with that of the Alexandrian Christians

Such is the effect of that iniquitous order which was issued by Constantius. On the part of the people there was displayed a ready alacrity to submit to martyrdom, and an increased hatred of this most impious heresy; and yet lamentations for their Churches, and groans burst from all, while they cried unto the Lord, 'Spare Your people, O Lord, and give not Your heritage unto Your enemies to reproach Joel 2:17;' but make haste to deliver us out of the hand of the lawless. For behold, 'they have not spared Your servants, but are preparing the way for Antichrist.' For the Meletians will never resist him, nor will they care for the truth, nor will they esteem it an evil thing to deny Christ. They are men who have not approached the word with sincerity; like the chameleon they assume every various appearance; they are hirelings of any who will make use of them. They make not the truth their aim, but prefer before it their present pleasure; they say only, 'Let us eat and drink, for tomorrow we die 1 Corinthians 15:32.' Such a profession and faithless temper is more worthy of Epicritian players than of Meletians. But the faithful servants of our Saviour, and the true Bishops who believe with sincerity, and live not for themselves, but for the Lord; these faithfully believing in our Lord

Jesus Christ, and knowing, as I said before, that the charges which were alleged against the truth were false, and plainly fabricated for the sake of the Arian heresy (for by the recantation of Ursacius and Valens they detected the calumnies which were devised against Athanasius, for the purpose of removing him out of the way, and of introducing into the Churches the impieties of the enemies of Christ); these, I say, perceiving all this, as defenders and preachers of the truth, chose rather, and endured to be insulted and driven into banishment, than to subscribe against him, and to hold communion with the Arian madmen. They forgot not the lessons they had taught to others; yea, they know well that great dishonour remains for the traitors, but for them which confess the truth, the kingdom of heaven; and that to the careless and such as fear Constantius will happen no good thing; but for them that endure tribulations here, as sailors reach a quiet haven after a storm, as wrestlers receive a crown after the combat, so these shall obtain great and eternal joy and delight in heaven;— such as Joseph obtained after those tribulations; such as the great Daniel had after his temptations and the manifold conspiracies of the courtiers against him; such as Paul now enjoys, being crowned by the Saviour; such as the people of God everywhere expect. They, seeing these things, were not infirm of purpose, but waxed strong in faith , and increased in their zeal more and more. Being fully persuaded of the calumnies and impieties of the heretics, they condemn the persecutor, and in heart and mind run together the same course with them that are persecuted, that they also may obtain the crown of Confession.

Duty of separating from heretics

One might say much more against this detestable and antichristian heresy, and might demonstrate by many arguments that the practices of Constantius are a prelude to the coming of Antichrist. But seeing that, as the Prophet Isaiah 1:6 has said, from the feet even to the head there is no reasonableness in it, but it is full of all filthiness and all impiety, so that the very name of it ought to be avoided as a dog's vomit or the poison of serpents; and seeing that Costyllius openly exhibits the image of the adversary 2 Thessalonians 2:4; in order that our words may not be too many, it will be well to content ourselves with the divine Scripture, and that we all obey the precept which it has given us both in regard to other heresies, and especially respecting this. That precept is as follows; 'Depart, depart, go out from thence, touch no unclean thing; go out of the midst of them, and be separate, that bear the vessels of the Lord Isaiah 52:11.' This may suffice to instruct us all, so that if any one has been deceived by them, he may go out from them, as out of Sodom, and not return again unto them, lest he suffer the fate of Lot's wife; and if any one has continued from the beginning pure from this impious heresy, he may glory in Christ and say, 'We have not stretched out our hands to a strange god ; neither have we worshipped the works of our own hands, nor served the creature more than You, the God that hast created all things through Your word, the Only-Begotten Son our Lord Jesus Christ, through whom to You the Father together with the same Word in the Holy Spirit be glory and power for ever and ever. Amen.'

The Second Protest

The people of the Catholic Church in Alexandria, which is under the government of the most Reverend Bishop Athanasius, make this public protest by those whose names are under-written.

We have already protested against the nocturnal assault which was committed upon ourselves and the Lord's house; although in truth there needed no protest in respect to proceedings with which the whole city has been already made acquainted. For the bodies of the slain which were discovered were exposed in public, and the bows and arrows and other arms found in the Lord's house loudly proclaim the iniquity.

But whereas after our Protest already made, the most illustrious Duke Syrianus endeavours to force all men to agree with him, as though no tumult had been made, nor any had perished (wherein is no small proof that these things were not done according to the wishes of the most gracious Emperor Augustus Constantius; for he would not have been so much afraid of the consequences of this transaction, had he acted therein by command); and whereas also, when we went to him, and requested him not to do violence to any, nor to deny what had taken place, he ordered us, being Christians, to be beaten with clubs; thereby again giving proof of the nocturnal assault which has been directed against the Church:—

We therefore make also this present Protest, certain of us being now about to travel to the most religious Emperor Augustus: and we adjure Maximus the Prefect of Egypt, and the Controllers , in the name of Almighty God, and for the sake of the salvation of the most religious Augustus Constantius, to relate all these things to the piety of Augustus, and to the authority of the most illustrious Prefects. We adjure also the masters of vessels, to publish these things everywhere, and to carry them to the ears of the most religious Augustus, and to the Prefects and the Magistrates in every place, in order that it may be known that a war has been waged against the Church, and that, in the times of Augustus Constantius, Syrianus has caused virgins and many others to become martyrs.

As it dawned upon the fifth before the Ides of February , that is to say, the fourteenth of the month Mechir, while we were keeping vigil in the Lord's house, and engaged in our prayers (for there was to be a communion on the Preparation); suddenly about midnight, the most illustrious Duke Syrianus attacked us and the Church with many legions of soldiers armed with naked swords and javelins and other warlike instruments, and wearing helmets on their heads; and actually while we were praying, and while the lessons were being read, they broke down the doors. And when the doors were burst open by the violence of the multitude, he gave command, and some of them were shooting; others shouting, their arms rattling, and their swords flashing in the light of the lamps; and immediately virgins were being slain, many men trampled down, and falling over one another as the soldiers came upon them, and several were pierced with arrows and perished. Some of the soldiers also were betaking themselves to plunder, and were stripping the virgins, who were more afraid of being even touched by them than they were of death. The Bishop continued sitting upon his throne, and exhorted all to pray. The Duke led on the attack, having with him Hilarius the notary, whose part in the proceedings was shown in the sequel. The Bishop was seized, and barely escaped being torn to pieces; and having fallen into a state of insensibility, and appearing as one dead, he disappeared from among them, and has gone we know not whither. They were eager to kill him. And when they saw that many had perished, they gave orders to the soldiers to remove out of sight the bodies of the dead. But the most holy virgins who were left behind were buried in the tombs, having attained the glory of martyrdom in the times of the most religious Constantius. Deacons also were beaten with stripes even in the Lord's house, and were shut up there.

Nor did matters stop even here: for after all this had happened, whosoever pleased broke open any door that he could, and searched, and plundered what was within. They entered even into those places which not even all Christians are allowed to enter. Gorgonius, the commander of the city force , knows this, for he was present. And no unimportant evidence of the nature of this hostile assault is afforded by the circumstance, that the armour and javelins and swords borne by those who entered were left in the Lord's house. They have been hung up in the Church until this time, that they might not be able to deny it: and although they sent several times Dynamius the soldier , as well as the Commander of the city police, desiring to take them away, we would not allow it, until the circumstance was known to all.

Now if an order has been given that we should be persecuted we are all ready to suffer martyrdom. But if it be not by order of Augustus, we desire Maximus the Prefect of Egypt and all the city magistrates to request of him that they may not again be suffered thus to assail us. And we desire also that this our petition may be presented to him, that they may not attempt to bring in hither any other Bishop: for we have resisted unto death , desiring to have the most Reverend Athanasius, whom God gave us at the beginning, according to the succession of our fathers; whom also the most religious Augustus Constantius himself sent to us with letters and oaths. And we believe that when his Piety is informed of what has taken place, he will be greatly displeased, and will do nothing contrary to his oaths, but will again give orders that our Bishop Athanasius shall remain with us.

To the Consuls to be elected after the Consulship of

the most illustrious Arbæthion and Collianus , on the seventeenth Mechir , which is the day before the Ides of February.

History of the arians ~ Athanasius of Alexandria

Limovia.net - classics of Christianity

Index

The author: Athanasius of Alexandria.........................3

BOOK I..**17**

Arian Persecution Under Constantine.......................17

Arianssacrifice morality and integrity to party.........19

Recklessness of their proceedings..............................21

Arianspersecute Eustathius and others......................23

Case of Marcellus...25

Martyrdom of Paul of Constantinople.......................26

Restoration of the Catholics......................................29

BOOK II..**30**

First Arian Persecution under Constantius...............30

Violent Intrusion of Gregory.....................................32

The Easterns decline the Council at Rome...............33

Cruelties of Gregory at Alexandria............................35

Profaneness of Gregory and death of Balacius.........36

BOOK III..38

Restoration of the Catholics on the Council of Sardica
....38

Secession of the Easterns at Sardica..........................41

Proceedings of the Council of Sardica.......................43

Arian Persecution after Sardica.................................45

Tyrannical measures against the Alexandrians.........46

Plot against the Catholic Legates at Antioch............48

Constantius' change of mind.....................................50

Athanasius visits Constantius...................................51

Constantius Augustus, the Great, the Conqueror, to the Bishops and Clergy of the Catholic Church.......53

The following is the letter which he wrote after the death of the blessed Constans. It was written in Latin, and is here translated into Greek..............................54

History of the arians ~ Athanasius of Alexandria

Return of Athanasius from second exile....................55

Recantation of Ursacius and Valens..........................57

Triumph of Athanasius..59

BOOK IV..60

Second ArianPersecution under Constantius............60

Relapse of Ursacius and Valens................................62

Constantius changes sides again...............................63

Constantius begins to persecute................................65

Persecution by Constantius.......................................67

Persecution is from the Devil....................................69

Banishment of the Western Bishops spread the knowledge of the truth...71

BOOK V...73

Persecution and Lapse of Liberius............................73

The Eunuch Eusebius attempts Liberius in vain.......75

Liberius refuses the Emperor's offering....................77

The evil influence of Eunuchs at Court............79

Liberius's speech to Constantius..............81

Banishment of Liberius and others............82

Lapse of Liberius.....................84

BOOK VI...............................**86**

Persecution and Lapse of Hosius............86

Brave resistance of Hosius.................88

'Hosius to Constantius the Emperor sends health in the Lord.'...................90

Lapse of Hosius, due to cruel persecution................94

Arbitrary expulsion of so many bishops............96

BOOK VII.............................**98**

Persecution at Alexandria.....................98

Attacks upon the Alexandrian Church............100

Hypocrisy of the pretended respect of Constantius for his brother's memory...............102

How Constantius shows his respect for his father and brother..104

The Emperor has no right to rule the Church.........106

Despotic interference of Constantius......................108

Constantius gives up the Alexandrian Churches to the heretics...109

Irruption into the great Church...............................111

The great Church pillaged.......................................113

General Persecution at Alexandria..........................116

Violence of Sebastianus...118

Martyrdom of Eutychius..119

Ill-treatment of the poor..121

Ill-treatment of the poor..123

Ill-treatment of the Presbyters and Deacons...........124

BOOK VIII..125

Persecution in Egypt..125

Martyrdom of Secundus of Barka............................127

Persecution the weapon of Arianism.......................129
Arianismworse than other heresies, because of
Persecution..131

Constantius worse than Saul, Ahab, and Pilate. His
past conduct to his own relations.............................133

Inconstancy of Constantius......................................136

This wickedness unprecedented...............................138

Banishment of Egyptian Bishops.............................140

Character of Ariannominees.....................................142

The Episcopal appointments of Constantius a mark of
Antichrist...143

Arrival of George at Alexandria, and proceedings of
Constantius in Italy...145

Tyrannous banishment of Bishops by Constantius. 147

Constantius the precursor of Antichrist...................149

Alliance of Meletians with Arians...........................151

Behaviour of the Meletians contrasted with that of the

Alexandrian Christians..153

Duty of separating from heretics.............................156

The Second Protest..158

Limovia.net - classics of Christianity

Look for other classics of Christianity on:
LIMOVIA.NET

THANK YOU!

Printed in Great Britain
by Amazon